Spanish Grammar for Beginners
Textbook + Workbook Included

Supercharge Your Spanish With Essential Lessons and Exercises

©All rights reserved 2022
MyDailySpanish.com

No part of this book including the audio material may be copied, reproduced, transmitted or distributed in any form without the prior written permission of the author. For permission requests, write to: support@mydailyspanish.com.

Also available:

- Spanish Short Stories for Beginners (https://geni.us/spanishbookbeginner)
- Spanish Short Stories for Intermediate Level (https://geni.us/spanintervol1)
- Spanish Phrase Book (https://geni.us/spanishphrase)

For more products by My Daily Spanish, please visit:

https://store.mydailyspanish.com/

Table of Contents

Introduction v

Advice on how to use this book effectively vii

Lesson 1: Greetings – Los saludos 1
   Workbook Lesson 1: Greetings – Los saludos 4

Lesson 2: Introductions, professions, countries, and nationalities – Presentarse, profesiones, países y nacionalidades. 7
   Workbook Lesson 2: Introductions, professions, countries, and nationalities – Presentarse, profesiones, países y nacionalidades. 13

Lesson 3: Pronunciation and the alphabet – Pronunciación y alfabeto 16
   Workbook Lesson 3: Pronunciation and the alphabet – Pronunciación y alfabeto .. 22

Lesson 4: Nouns – Sustantivos 24
   Workbook Lesson 4: Nouns – Sustantivos 28

Lesson 5: Numbers – Los números 31
   Workbook Lesson 5: Numbers – Los números 37

Lesson 6: Verb conjugations – Conjugaciones verbales 40
   Workbook Lesson 6: Verb conjugations – Conjugaciones verbales 51

Lesson 7: "There is"/"There are" – Hay 54
   Workbook Lesson 7: "There is"/"There are" – Hay 57

Lesson 8: Present tense – El presente simple 60
   Workbook Lesson 8: Present tense – El presente simple 71

Lesson 9: The past tense – El pasado 74
   Workbook Lesson 9: The past tense – El pasado 80

Lesson 10: The future tense – El futuro 83
   Workbook Lesson 10: Future tense – El futuro 89

Lesson 11: Asking questions – Hacer preguntas 92
   Workbook Lesson 11: Asking questions – Hacer preguntas 96

Lesson 12: The verbs "to be" – Ser y estar 99
   Workbook Lesson 12: The verbs "to be" – Ser y estar 106

Lesson 13: Singular and plural nouns – Sustantivos singulares y plurales 109

   Workbook Lesson 13: Singular and plural nouns – Sustantivos singulares y plurales 114

Lesson 14: Adjectives – Adjetivos 117

   Workbook Lesson 14: Adjectives – Adjetivos 122

Lesson 15: How to tell time – Cómo dar la hora. 125

   Workbook Lesson 15: How to tell time – Cómo decir la hora 133

Lesson 16: Negatives – La negación 135

   Workbook Lesson 16: Negatives – La negación 140

Lesson 17: Prepositions – Preposiciones. 143

   Workbook Lesson 17: Prepositions – Preposiciones 148

Lesson 18: When to use "por" vs. "para" 151

   Workbook lesson 18: When to use "por" vs. "para". 158

Lesson 19: Perfect tense – Tiempo perfecto. 161

   Workbook Lesson 19: Perfect tense – Tiempo perfecto. 166

Lesson 20: Possessives – Posesivos. 169

   Workbook Lesson 20: Possessives – Posesivos 175

Lesson 21: Demonstrative adjectives and demonstrative pronouns – Adjetivos demostrativos y pronombres demostrativos 178

   Workbook lesson 21: Demonstrative adjectives and demonstrative pronouns – Adjetivos demostrativos y pronombres demostrativos. 184

Lesson 22: Making comparisons – Hacer comparaciones 187

   Workbook Lesson 22: Making comparisons – Hacer comparaciones. 195

Conclusion 198

How to Download the Free Audio Files? 199

About My Daily Spanish. 200

A Complete Audio Method for Spanish Language Learning 201

Introduction

When learning any language, grammar definitely comes up as the most challenging – and boring – part. Spanish is no different. Unfortunately, grammar is not something that can just be relegated to the sidelines.

You simply cannot skip the grammar if you truly want to become proficient. There are no shortcuts. If you want to be able to express yourself in Spanish using clear and precise language, you need to build a solid foundation in Spanish grammar.

This book is here to help you. In this book, we will lay down the rules of Spanish grammar and provide you with lots of examples, explanations, and exercises.

Practice Your Spanish Listening Skills and Pronunciation

A key to success in language learning is to get a good grasp of pronunciation at the beginning of your lessons. This requires constant listening practice. With this book's audio accompaniment, you will get a head start in your listening comprehension as well as honing your pronunciation from the start.

Each lesson and exercise contains audio narrated by native Spanish speakers. By listening to the audio and reading the written text at the same time, you will be able to connect how the Spanish words and sentences appear with how they sound when spoken in actual Spanish conversations.

Embedded Grammar Workbook

You don't need to buy a separate workbook to help you practice the grammar points you learn. We've integrated hundreds of different exercises in the book so you'll be able to cement your learning by taking the quizzes after each lesson and you'll be able to assess your progress as you go along.

Build a Learning Habit

This book also aims to help you build a learning habit that will sustain your Spanish learning even if your motivation wanes as you go along. You'll find that the book is divided into 22 lessons with one lesson meant to be tackled each day. After 22 days of studying consistently every day, you will have formed a learning habit that will ultimately help you achieve your learning goals.

Spanish Grammar, Simplified

Spanish grammar is already complicated enough so, in this book, you'll notice that we use the simplest yet most thorough explanations. We do not want to burden you with wordy explanations and unnecessary jargon. Instead, in this book we explain Spanish grammar in a way that makes it easily digestible and easy to grasp.

We've put a lot of effort into designing this book in a way that will be most useful to your Spanish language learning journey. We certainly hope that it will help you build the strong grammar foundation you need to reach fluency in Spanish.

Thank you very much and good luck.

My Daily Spanish Team

Advice on how to use this book effectively

This book is divided into 22 lessons and one lesson is meant to be followed each day for around 30 minutes to an hour.

If a lesson seems too long for you, you can tackle the lesson over two days. The important thing is that you work on it every day for 22 days (or more) so that it helps you build an effective learning habit.

Thank you,

My Daily Spanish Team

Important! The link to download the Audio Files is available at the end of this book. (Page 199)

Lesson 1: Greetings – Los saludos

The first thing you need to know about a new language is how to greet people. For our first lesson today, we'll learn how to say "hello" as well as other greetings in Spanish.

Let's start!

Listen to Track 1

Basic Spanish Greetings

¡Hola! – Hello!

Buenos días – Good morning.

Buenas tardes – Good afternoon.

Buenas noches – Good evening.

¿Cómo está? – How are you? (formal)

¿Cómo está usted? – How are you? (formal)

¿Cómo estás? – How are you? (informal)

¿Cómo están? – How are you? (informal/formal plural)

Buenas – Hello. (You'll hear this a lot on the streets, or when you walk into shops, etc.)

¿Qué tal? / ¿Cómo andas? – How are you doing? / What's up? (very informal)

¿Qué hay? / ¿Qué onda? – (Loosely translated) What's up? (Also very informal – use only with friends, family, etc.)

Common Responses

Listen to Track 2

You can reply with:

Bien, gracias – I'm good, thank you.

Bien, gracias, ¿y usted? – Good, thanks, and you? (formal)

Bien, gracias, ¿y tú? – Good, thanks, and you? (informal)

Más o menos – So-so. / Not so good.

Como siempre – As always.

Todo bien – Everything's good.

Muy bien – Very good.

Aquí estamos – Here we are. (It's like saying "still here, alive and kicking")

Estoy de maravilla – I'm great!

As well as saying "hello," you need to be able to say "goodbye." Let's have a look at the different ways to say this in Spanish.

Saying Goodbye in Spanish

Listen to Track 3

Adiós – Goodbye

Bye – Goodbye

Chao – Bye (informal)

Nos vemos – See you (informal)

Hasta mañana – See you tomorrow

Hasta luego – See you later.

Hasta la próxima semana – See you next week.

Que tengas un buen día – Have a nice day.

Hasta pronto – See you soon.

You've made a great start! See you again tomorrow for a really long lesson on how to introduce yourself in Spanish. *¡Hasta la próxima!*

Informal Conversation in Spanish

Listen to Track 4

María: ¡Hola!

Andrés: ¡Hola! ¿Cómo estás?

María: Bien, gracias, ¿y tú?

Andrés: Muy bien.

María: Nos vemos.

Andrés: Hasta pronto.

Translation:

María: Hello!

Andrés: Hello! How are you?

María: Good, thanks, and you?

Andrés: Very good.

María: See you.

Andrés: See you soon.

Formal Conversation in Spanish

Listen to Track 5

María: ¡Buenos días, ¿cómo está usted?

Profesora González: ¡Buenos días! Bien, gracias, ¿y tú?

María: Bien, gracias. Nos vemos mañana en clase.

Profesora González: ¡Hasta mañana! Que tengas un buen día.

María: Gracias, igual usted.

Translation:

María: Good morning, how are you?

Professor González: Good morning! I'm good, thanks, and you?

María: I'm good, thanks. See you tomorrow in class.

Professor González: See you tomorrow! Have a nice day.

María: Thanks, you as well.

Workbook Lesson 1: Greetings – Los saludos

Exercise 1: Tick the right answer.

1- Camila is a friend of María's. She would ask her:
   a. ¿Cómo estás?   b. ¿Cómo está usted?

2- Pedro wants to say good morning to Andrés. He would say:
   a. Buenas tardes.   b. Buenos días.   c. Buenas noches.

3- To wish someone a good night, you would say:
   a. Buenos días.   b. Buenas tardes.   c. Buenas noches.

4- To say goodbye, you should say:
   a. Hola   b. ¿Cómo estás?   c. Hasta luego.

5- You want to ask your boss how he is. You say:
   a. ¿Cómo estás?   b. ¿Cómo está usted?

Exercise 2: Translate from Spanish to English and vice versa.

Spanish	English
1- *¡Buenos días!*	
2-	How are you? (informal)
3-	Well, thank you.
4- *Muy bien.*	
5-	And you? (informal)
6- *Nos vemos.*	

Exercise 3: Translate this conversation from English to Spanish.

You: Good morning. How's it going?

Your friend: Good. And you?

You: Everything is going well. See you soon!

Your friend: Bye!

Exercise 4: Tick the right answer.

1- Your friend asked you "¿Cómo estás?" You're not feeling very well, so you would say:

   a. Muy bien.   b. De maravilla.   c. No muy bien.

2- To wish someone a good day, you would say:

   a. Buenas tardes.   b. Buenas noches.   c. Buenos días.

3- You've been talking to a friend and you want to say "See you soon" before going your separate ways. You would say:

   a. ¡Hasta pronto!   b. ¡Hasta luego!   c. ¡Hola!

4- You're talking to your boss. You say:

   a. Yo estoy bien, gracias. Y ¿tú?
   b. Yo estoy bien, gracias. Y ¿usted?

5- How would you answer if somebody asked you "¿Cómo estás?":

   a. Muy bien, gracias.   b. ¡Hola!   c. Hasta pronto.

Exercise 5: Translate from Spanish to English and vice versa.

Spanish	English
	Hello!/Hi! (informal)
	How are you? (formal)
3- *Todo va bien.*	
	Bye! (informal)
5- *Buenas noches.*	
6- *Buenas tardes.*	

Answers:

Exercise 1

1/ ¿Cómo estás? 2/ Buenos días 3/ Buenas noches 4/ Hasta luego 5/ ¿Cómo está usted?

Exercise 2

1/ Good morning! / Hello! 2/ ¿Cómo estás? 3/ Bien, gracias. 4/ Very well. 5/ ¿Y tú? 6/ See you.

Exercise 3

Tú: Buenos días, ¿cómo estás?
Tu amigo: Bien. Y ¿tú?
Tú: Todo va bien. ¡Hasta pronto!
Tu amigo: Chao

Exercise 4

1/ No muy bien. 2/ Buenos días. 3/ ¡Hasta pronto! 4/ Yo estoy bien, gracias. Y ¿usted? 5/ Muy bien, gracias.

Exercise 5

1/ ¡Hola! 2/ ¿Cómo está? - ¿Cómo está usted? 3/ Everything is going well. 4/ Chao 5/ Good night. 6/ Good afternoon.

Lesson 2: Introductions, professions, countries, and nationalities – Presentarse, profesiones, países y nacionalidades

One of the first things you need to know is how to start a conversation in Spanish. If you can't make a start, how are you ever going to practice? And what better way to start a conversation than by introducing yourself?

Here, you'll find some quick tips, phrases, and different ways of introducing yourself in Spanish to get the conversational ball rolling.

Getting Started

Let's look at the very basics of how you'll go about letting the Spanish speaking world know just who you are.

In the previous lesson we talked about how to greet someone in Spanish. Using the greetings you've learned, you can already begin the conversation. Then you move on to....

Yo me llamo...

Listen to Track 6

The logical next step, after saying "hello" to someone, would be to tell them your name! Once again, you have some options.

(Yo) me llamo... - The most commonly used expression, and literally translated it means "I call myself..."

Soy*... - If you like brevity, this introduction is for you! It's like saying "I'm..."

Mi nombre es... - The very practical "My name is..."

*This verb (which comes from *ser*, one of the two ways in Spanish to say "to be") will come in handy when introducing yourself, so make sure you keep it in the back of your mind, as we'll be seeing it again.

Getting Deeper

While it is important to know someone's name to strike up a conversation with them, if that's all you say, the chat will be very short-lived. So, what else can you say about yourself?

Listen to Track 7

Soy de... Vivo en...

The verb *soy* was mentioned before and means "I am...." If you add the (very useful) preposition *de* after it, you're saying "I am from....".

Soy de Chicago – I am from Chicago.

Just because you're from somewhere, doesn't necessarily mean that you live there. So, that's probably a good little piece of information to give someone about yourself. You can say *vivo en* (I live in...)

Soy de Chicago, pero vivo en Chile – I'm from Chicago, but I live in Chile.

Tengo *X* años.

Saying your age is a little different. Surprisingly, you don't use *ser* or *estar* for this one. Pay attention here, because this is something that really catches a lot of English speakers out. In Spanish, you are not 20 years old ... you *have* 20 years!

Tengo 20 años – I have 20 years. (Meaning - I am 20 years old.)

Listen to Track 8

Soy...

Another important thing you should be able to mention about yourself is what you do, as in "what's your job?"

Soy estudiante / profesor(a) / abogado(a) / dentista – I am a student / teacher / lawyer / dentist. Notice that the first and last of these examples don't change gender. More on gendered professions below.

Listen to Track 9

Me gusta...

Another useful expression you may want to know when introducing/talking about yourself is "me gusta...," which means "I like...." It's a tricky expression for English speakers because its construction is a little different from how it's said in English. Literally translated it means "To me X is pleasing...."

To keep it simple, let's stick with using this structure with some verbs in the infinitive, so we can say "To me (verb) is pleasing."

Me gusta leer / jugar basket / cocinar / ir al cine – I like to read / play basketball / cook / go to the movies.

Examples

Let's take everything we've seen and put it all together. Below you will find two examples of people introducing themselves. They are both native English speakers who live/study in Mexico. They will use the phrases we've mentioned, as well as adding in a few extra things about themselves.

Self-introduction in Spanish: Example 1

Listen to Track 10

> *¡Buenos días! Soy la profesora Ana González. Tengo veintisiete años. Soy de Chicago, pero ahora vivo en una ciudad en México que se llama Guadalajara. Soy profesora de inglés en una preparatoria. Al volver a Estados Unidos, voy a continuar con mis estudios.*

Translation:

Good morning! I'm professor Ana González. I'm 27 years old. I'm from Chicago, but now I live in a city in Mexico called Guadalajara. I'm an English teacher in a high school. When I return to the United States, I'm going to continue my studies.

Self-introduction in Spanish: Example 2

Listen to Track 11

> *Hola, me llamo Nick Schultz y soy de Estados Unidos. Vivo en México y soy profesor de inglés. Tengo veintiséis años. Estoy casado con una profesora que se llama Ana y tenemos un pequeño perro cuyo nombre es Joey. Llevo 8 años estudiando español.*

Translation:

Hello, my name is Nick Schultz and I'm from the United States. I live in Mexico and am an English teacher. I'm 26 years old. I am married to a professor named Ana and we have a little dog whose name is Joey. I have been studying Spanish for 8 years.

Let's dive deeper into occupations, nationalities, and countries in the next section. Ready?

Let's Talk About Jobs and Professions in Spanish

When talking to new acquaintances or friends, jobs often come up. To ask about what someone does for a living, you can use one of the following:

Listen to Track 12

- *¿Cuál es tu trabajo/profesión?* (What is your job/profession?)
- *¿En qué trabajas?* (What do you work in?)
- *¿Qué haces?/ ¿A qué te dedicas?* (What do you do?)

To respond, you say:

- *Soy _____.* (I'm a _____.)

Including gender in professions in Spanish:

Listen to Track 13

- As a general rule, Spanish nouns pertaining to professions change according to the gender of the person they are referring to.
- Most profession nouns have masculine forms that end in o. To change it to feminine, simply replace the o with a. For example, *un maestro* becomes *una maestra*.
- Some profession nouns are exempted from this rule. This includes *un/una atleta* (athlete), *un/una piloto* (pilot), *un/una policía* (police), and *un/una modelo* (model) which remain the same whether masculine or feminine.
- For profession nouns that end in a consonant, just add an *a* to make it feminine. Example: *una profesora, una bailarina*.
- There are profession nouns that change a lot in spelling when converted to their feminine form. For example, *un alcalde* (mayor) becomes *una alcaldesa*.

Listen to Track 14

abogado (a)	lawyer
bombero (a)	fireman
contador (a)	accountant
dentista	dentist
enfermero (a)	nurse
estudiante	student
fotógrafo (a)	photographer
geólogo (a)	geologist
ingeniero (a)	engineer
jardinero (a)	gardener

Lesson 2: Introductions, professions, countries, and nationalities – Presentarse, profesiones, países y nacionalidades

médico (a) - doctor (a)	doctor
niñera (o)	nanny
obrero (a)	laborer
profesor (a)	teacher
químico (a)	chemist
reportero (a)	reporter
soldado	soldier
técnico (a)	technician
vendedor (a)	salesman
zapatero (a)	shoemaker

Countries and Nationalities in Spanish

When introducing yourself or getting to know someone, your country of origin and nationality are bound to come up as a topic. In this section, let's talk about what the different countries and nationalities are called in Spanish.

You should also know that, unlike English, Spanish doesn't capitalize nationalities. Country names are capitalized just as in English, but nationalities don't need to be capitalized.

Here's a sample conversation:

Listen to Track 15

Andrés: *¿De dónde eres?* – Where are you from?

Camila: *Soy de Estados Unidos. Soy americana/estadounidense. Y tú, ¿de dónde eres?* – I'm from the United States. I'm American. And you, where are you from?

Andrés: *Yo soy de México, pero vivo en Brasil. Soy fotógrafo.* – I'm from Mexico, but I live in Brazil. I'm a photographer.

Camila: *¡Qué bien! Yo soy estudiante.* – How cool! I am a student.

Now let's look at a formal conversation:

Listen to Track 16

Pedro: *¿De dónde es usted?* – Where are you from?

Profesor Schultz: *Soy de Estados Unidos. Soy profesor de inglés. Y tú, ¿de dónde eres?* – I'm from the United States. I'm an English professor. And you, where are you from?

Pedro: *Yo soy de Guatemala. Soy guatemalteco, pero vivo en Guadalajara.* Soy enfermero. – I'm from Guatemala. I'm Guatemalan, but I live in Guadalajara. I'm a nurse.

Countries and Nationalities in Spanish:

Listen to Track 17

- Argentina – argentino (a)
- Australia – australiano (a)
- Brasil – brasileño (a)
- Canadá – canadiense
- Colombia – colombiano (a)
- España – español (a)
- Estados Unidos – americano (a)/ estadounidense
- Guatemala – guatemalteco (a)
- Inglaterra – inglés, inglesa
- México – mexicano (a)

Some notes:

Listen to Track 18

- When talking about nationalities in Spanish, nationality adjectives are used. These can take four forms: masculine singular, feminine singular, masculine plural, and feminine plural. For example: *francés* (masculine singular), *francesa* (feminine singular), *franceses* (masculine plural), and *francesas* (feminine plural).
- Nationalities that end in 'e' or an accented vowel have the same masculine or feminine singular form. For example: *iraquí, israelí,* and *iraní.*

Workbook Lesson 2: Introductions, professions, countries, and nationalities – Presentarse, profesiones, países y nacionalidades

Exercise 1: Fill in the blanks with the correct word/phrases to complete the following sentences.

1- _____ Pedro. (My name is Pedro.)
2- _____ abogado. (I am a lawyer.)
3- _____ de Chicago. (I am from Chicago.)
4- _____ 20 años. (I am 20 years old.)
5- Ella _____ arquitecta. (She is an architect.)

Exercise 2: Complete the table with nationalities in feminine singular and masculine/feminine plural.

| Singular || Plural ||
Masculino	Femenino	Masculino	Femenino
brasileño	1-	2-	3-
inglés	4-	ingleses	5-
estadounidense	6-	7-	estadounidenses
australiano	8-	9-	10-
guatemalteco	11-	12-	13-

Exercise 3: Complete the following sentences with nationalities in masculine or feminine, singular or plural form.

1- El real es la moneda _____ . (The real is the Brazilian currency.)
2- Gabriel García Márquez es un escritor _____. (Gabriel García Márquez is a Colombian writer.)
3- Buenos Aires es una ciudad _____. (Buenos Aires is an Argentine city.)
4- Pedro es un chico _____. (Pedro is a Guatemalan guy.)
5- Julia Roberts es una actriz _____. (Julia Roberts is an American actress.)

Exercise 4: Tick the right answer.

1- Yo____ llamo Pedro. (My name is Pedro.)
   a. me   b. te   c. se

2- Él es _____ . (He is Mexican.)
   a. mexicano   b. mexicana   c. mexican

3- Yo ____ 21 años. (I am 21 years old.)
   a. tengo   b. llamo   c. soy

4- ____ de Australia. (I am from Australia.)
   a. Soy   b. Somos   c. Es

5- Me ____ el té. (I like tea.)
   a. gustan   b. gusta   c. llamo

Exercise 5: Translate the following text from Spanish to English.

Hola, me llamo Sara y soy de Canadá. Vivo en Francia y soy profesora de inglés. Tengo treinta años. Tengo un novio que se llama Pierre y un pequeño gato cuyo nombre es Pete.

Exercise 6: Complete the following phrases with professions.

1- Nick es _____ . (Nick is a teacher.)
2- El señor García es _____. (Mr García is a garbage collector.)
3- Él es _____. (He is a carpenter.)
4- Antonio es _____. (Antonio is a butcher.)
5- Pedro es_____. (Pedro is a scientist.)

Exercise 7: Translate the following text from Spanish to English.

1- Luis es argentino, vive en Buenos Aires.
2- Las pirámides mayas son mexicanas.
3- Los colombianos son amables.
4- Me gusta el café brasileño.
5- Sara vive en Madrid, pero es canadiense.

Answers:

Exercise 1

1/ Mi nombre es 2/ Soy 3/ Soy 4/ Tengo 5/ es

Exercise 2

1/ brasileña 2/ brasileños 3/ brasileñas 4/ inglesa 5/ inglesas 6/ estadounidense 7/ estadounidenses 8/ australiana 9/ australianos 10/ australianas 11/ guatemalteca 12/ guatemaltecos 13/ guatemaltecas

Exercise 3

1/ brasileña 2/ colombiano 3/ argentina 4/ guatemalteco 5/ estadounidense

Exercise 4

1/ me 2/ mexicano 3/ tengo 4/ Soy 5/ gusta

Exercise 5

Hi, my name is Sara and I'm from Canada. I live in France and I'm an English teacher. I'm 30. I have a boyfriend named Pierre and a little cat whose name is Pete.

Exercise 6

1/ profesor 2/ recolector de basura 3/ carpintero 4/ carnicero 5/ científico

Exercise 7

1/ Luis is Argenitinian. He lives in Buenos Aires. 2/ The Mayan pyramids are Mexican. 3/ Colombians are kind. 4/ I like Brazilian coffee. 5/ Sara lives in Madrid, but she's Canadian.

Lesson 3: Pronunciation and the alphabet – Pronunciación y alfabeto

Spanish is a fairly easy language, considering that most Spanish words are pronounced exactly how they're spelt. It's not like English where some of the pronunciations are absurd.

That being said, there are some tips and tricks to have you sounding like a local in no time. So sit back, grab a *cerveza* (pronounced ser-beh-sah) and let this book be your guide.

Let's start off with an important Spanish pronunciation tip...

In Spanish, a really important thing to notice and remember is which syllable to stress.

I remember getting into a cab in Mexico and feeling nervous when the cabbie didn't recognize the street I was asking him to go to. When I showed him the street name on my phone, he was quick to correct me and say that I had stressed the wrong syllable – and that small mistake had prevented him from understanding me at all.

But ... don't stress about the stress!

There are some simple rules that you can memorize so that you always know which syllable you need to stress.

Some General Rules to Follow on Stressing Syllables:

Listen to Track 19

- **If a word ends in a vowel or "n" or "s," you need to stress the syllable that is next to the last one.**

    Por ejemplo (for example):
    Cuenta (the bill at a restaurant) is pronounced <u>kwen</u>-tah.
    Examen (test/exam) is pronounced ex-<u>ah</u>-men.
    Pestaña (eyelash) is pronounced pez-<u>tah</u>-nya.

- **Words that end in a consonant (other than "n" or "s") are stressed on the last syllable.**

    Por ejemplo: Comer (to eat) is pronounced koh-<u>mehr.</u>

- **When there is an accent above a letter, you must stress that syllable.**

    Por ejemplo: Próximo (next) is pronounced <u>prohk</u>-see-moh.

See, that was easy. Feeling a little less stressed now? Let's move on to vowels!

Spanish Pronunciation Guide: How to Pronounce Spanish Vowels

The sounds the vowels make in spoken Spanish very seldom change. That's great for learners because it means you need only memorize this Spanish pronunciation guide for vowels below.

So, if you're sounding out a word and you use these vowel pronunciations, there is a very good chance you've got it right!

Listen to Track 20

Vowel	Pronunciation Guide	Example	What the Example Means
A	is pronounced "a" like cat.	*Abajo*	Down/Downstairs
E	is pronounced "eh" like rent.	*Antes*	Before
I	is pronounced "ee" like free.	*Amigo*	Friend
O	is pronounced "oh" like flow.	*Beso*	Kiss
U	is pronounced "oo" like loose.	*Nube (noob-eh)*	Cloud
AI/AY	is pronounced "ar" like fly.	*Bailar /Hay (eye)*	Dance/There Is
AU	is pronounced "ow" like how.	*Aunque*	Although
EI	is pronounced "ay" like day.	*Aceite*	Oil
IE	is pronounced "yeh" like yes.	*Bien*	Fine
UE	is pronounced "weh" like well.	*Cuello*	Neck/Collar

The (Usually) Constant Spanish Consonants and How to Say Them

Most of the consonants in Spanish are pronounced the same as in English. However, there are some that are different, and they can seem a little intimidating at first.

We've listed all of the ones that vary from English below.

Listen to Track 21

Consonant	Pronunciation Guide	Example	What the Example Means
C (before "e," "i")	is pronounced "s" like silk (in Castilian Spanish it would be "th" like thanks).	*Gracias/Cena*	thank you/dinner
C (before "a," "o," "u")	is pronounced "k" like corner.	*Casa/Con/Cuando*	house/with/when
CC	is pronounced "ks."	*Dirección*	address
D (between vowels)	is pronounced "th" like the.	*Cada*	each
G (before "a," "o," "u")	is pronounced as a hard "g" like grape.	*Gris*	gray
G (before "e," "i")	is pronounced as a breathy "h" like hi.	*Gente (hehn-teh)*	people
H	is not pronounced. Always silent.	*Hay (eye)*	there is
J	is pronounced as a breathy "h" like hot.	*Jamón*	ham
L	is pronounced like "l" in love.	*Libre*	free
LL	is pronounced as a hard "j" like Jacob.	*Llamar*	to call
Ñ	is pronounced "ny" like canyon.	*Mañana*	tomorrow
QU	is pronounced "k" like keep.	*Queso (keh-soh)*	cheese
R	is rolled only once.	*Pero (pehr-oh)*	but
RR	is rolled twice.	*Perro (pehr-roh)*	dog
V	is pronounced "b" like beer.	*Vale (ball-eh)*	okay

X	is pronounced "cs" like exit.	*Extranjero*	foreign
Y	is pronounced like English "y" in yard, except when by itself it is pronounced "ee."	*Ya (yah)/Y (ee)*	already/and
Z	is pronounced "s" like salt (in Castilian Spanish it would be "th" like think).	*Zapato*	shoe

Important things to note about Spanish consonant pronunciation

Listen to Track 22

The letters "B" and "V" are pronounced the same – like "B" in bad. This makes it difficult for Spanish learners to sound out words in their writing.

To further explain the tricky CC listed above, the example given, *dirección*, is pronounced like dee-rek-see-on. So, the first "c" behaves just as we expect and the second is pronounced like "s."

When you pronounce the letter "J," it should almost sound like you're trying to clear your throat. If it doesn't almost hurt your throat, you're not doing it right.

Inside a word, the letter "M" will appear before "P" or "B," but "N" will not. Think "*limpiar*" (to clean) or "*hombre*" (man). That also happens when you pronounce two words where one finishes in "N" and the next starts with "P" or "B." For example, when saying "*con permiso*" ("excuse me," when trying to get by someone) it is pronounced like "compermiso." So, the "N" becomes "M."

I actually didn't notice this before I started learning Spanish, but in English the letter "L" has two different sounds. The first is the obvious – "L" like in "love." The second is less obvious. If you say the word "ball," you have the second "L" pronunciation. It's a bit softer than the first. That double "L" sound doesn't appear in Spanish so always go with the first!

¿What's with the upside down question marks?

When you're reading something in English, you generally know that it's a question before you get to the question mark at the end because of the word at the beginning. *Por ejemplo*: "Do you want something?"

I'm assuming that when reading that question, you put an upward inflection on it. That's because the word "do" tipped you off that it was a question and not a statement. Well, in Spanish you generally don't have a word clue but you do have a punctuation clue.

"Tú quieres algo." / "¿ Tú quieres algo?"

The first is a statement: "You want something." The second is a question: "Do you want something?"

The only way to tell the difference is by the punctuation. So, if you were reading the question, and there wasn't an inverted question mark at the beginning, you wouldn't know that it was a question until you got to the end.

The same goes for when you're speaking. It's super important to make sure that when asking a question, the inflection of your voice goes up.

It has to be clearly different from the inflection you use when making a statement. If not, you could end up saying something different from what you intended.

Hopefully, this Spanish pronunciation guide has helped you navigate through all the pronunciation confusion. Keep listening and reading – you'll get there!

The Spanish Alphabet

The Spanish language officially has 27 letters in its alphabet or *abecedario,* just one letter more than in English. The extra letter is *la letra ñ (eñe)* which doesn't exist in the English alphabet.

This updated Spanish alphabet was implemented by the *Real Academia Española* in 2010. Before that, the old Spanish dictionaries had sections for the now-defunct letters *ch* and *ll*. Other old resources would also previously include *rr* as another separate letter. Some would exclude the letters *k* and *w* because they only appear in words borrowed from other languages.

Lesson 3: Pronunciation and the alphabet – Pronunciación y alfabeto

In this lesson, we're going to get to know the 27 different letters in the Spanish alphabet.

Listen to Track 23

Letter	What It's Called in Spanish	How to Pronounce Its Spanish Name
Aa	*A*	AH
Bb	*Be*	BEH
Cc	*Ce*	SEH
Dd	*De*	DEH
Ee	*E*	EH
Ff	*Efe*	EH-feh
Gg	*Ge*	JEH
Hh	*Hache*	AH-cheh
Ii	*I*	EE
Jj	*Jota*	JOH-tah
Kk	*Ka*	KAH
Ll	*Ele*	EH-leh
Mm	*Eme*	EH-meh
Nn	*Ene*	EH-neh
Ññ	*Eñe*	EH-nyeh
Oo	*O*	OH
Pp	*Pe*	PEH
Qq	*Cu*	COO
Rr	*Erre*	EH-rreh
Ss	*Ese*	EH-seh
Tt	*Te*	TEH
Uu	*U*	OOH
Vv	*Uve*	OOH-beh
Ww	*doble uve (also known previously as "uve doble," "doble ve," and "doble u")*	DOH-bleh OOH
Xx	*Equis*	EH-kees
Yy	*ye (often referred to as i griega)*	YEH
Zz	*Zeta*	SEH-tah

Workbook Lesson 3: Pronunciation and the alphabet – Pronunciación y alfabeto

Exercise 1: Write the following letters to spell out a Spanish word and try to find out what each word means.

1- Uve, a, ce, a
2- Ce, a, erre, ele, o, ese
3- Ene, i, eñe, o
4- Jota, a, erre, de, i, ene
5- Te, e, ele, e, uve, i, ese, i, o, ene
6- Hache, a, be, ele, a, erre

Exercise 2: Spell the following names in Spanish.

1- ¿Cómo se llama? — Nick Schultz.
¿Puedes deletrearme el apellido? (Can you spell his surname?)

2- ¿Cómo se llama? —Pierre. (What's his name? —Pierre.)
¿Cómo se escribe? (How's it written?)

3- ¿Cómo se llama? — Camila. (What's her name? — Camila.)
¿Y de apellido? —Herrera. (And her surname? —Herrera.)
¿Cómo se escribe? (How's it written?)

Exercise 3: Write the letter next to the sound.

1- Hache
2- Ge
3- Eñe
4- Erre
5- Equis

Exercise 4: Write the letters to spell out the following professions, and try to find out what each word means.

1- Ce, a, ene, t, a, ene, te, e
2- Te, e, ce, ene, i, ce, o
3- Uve, e, te, e, erre, i, ene, a, erre, i, o
4- Zeta, a, pe, a, te, e, erre, o
5- Ese, a, ese, te, erre, e

Answers:

Exercise 1

1/ Vaca 2/ Carlos 3/ Niño 4/ Jardín 5/ Televisión 6/ Hablar

Exercise 2

1/ ese, ce, hache, u, ele, te, zeta 2/ pe, i, erre, erre, e 3/ hache, e, erre, erre, e, erre, a

Exercise 3

1/ h 2/ g 3/ ñ 4/ r 5/ x

Exercise 4

1/ Cantante 2/ Técnico 3/ Veterinario 4/ Zapatero 5/ Sastre

Lesson 4: Nouns – Sustantivos

This lesson is about nouns, such an important part of a sentence.

What are Spanish Nouns?

Spanish nouns, like their counterparts in all other languages, can either be a person, a place, a thing, or an idea.

Quick exercise

Listen to Track 24

Can you identify which of the words in the following Spanish conversation are nouns?

    María: *Bienvenido a mi casa.* (Welcome to my house.)

    Pedro: *Gracias.* (Thank you.)

    María: *Vamos a la sala. Ahí tengo unas sillas y la televisión. Podemos ver algo. La comida está en la cocina. Todavía está en el refrigerador.* (Let's go to the living room. There, I have some chairs and a television. We can watch something. The food is in the kitchen. It's still in the fridge.)

    Pedro: *¿Dónde está el baño?* (Where is the bathroom?)

    María: *Hay dos baños en mi casa. Uno está aquí y el otro está cerca de la sala.* (There are two bathrooms in my house. One is here, and the other is near the living room.)

Here are the answers:

María, casa, Pedro, sala, sillas, televisión, comida, cocina, refrigerador, baño, baños, casa, sala.

    María: *Bienvenido a mi **casa**.*

    Pedro: *Gracias.*

    María: *Vamos a la **sala**. Ahí tengo unas **sillas** y la **televisión**. Podemos ver algo. La **comida** está en la **cocina**. Todavía está en el **refrigerador**.*

    Pedro: *¿Dónde está el **baño**?*

    María: *Hay dos **baños** en mi **casa**. Uno está aquí, y el otro está cerca de la **sala**.*

Did you find all of the nouns?

Let's move on.

Spanish Noun Genders

Listen to Track 25

Did you notice in the short exercise above that each Spanish noun comes with a different article before it?

Why is it **la** *televisión* and **la** *cocina* while it's **el** *refrigerador* and **el** *baño*?

Say hello to Spanish noun genders!

Here are more examples:

Mesa – table (feminine)

Perro – dog (masculine)

Libro – book (masculine)

Casa – house (feminine)

Now it may be confusing for new learners, but after a bit of exposure to this lesson, you'll understand that there is, in fact, a system to it.

Here are some basic rules to remember on Spanish noun genders.

Generally speaking, words that end in -*o* are masculine (*perro/libro*), and, generally, words that end in -*a* are feminine (*mesa/casa*).

Seems simple enough! But be careful, because there are Spanish nouns that don't end in -*o* or -*a*. What about those?

In several cases, you'll be able to identify masculine or feminine nouns based on the gender associated with the word. Such as:

Listen to Track 26

Mujer – woman (feminine)

Hombre – man (masculine)

But some of the word genders just don't seem easy to figure out.

Additional rules

Masculine

Ends in -o

Ends in an accented vowel (á, é, í, ó, ú)

Ends in -ma (be careful with this one!)

Ends in a consonant that isn't -d or -z

Ends in -e

Feminine

Ends in -a

Ends in -sión or -ción

Ends in -dad or -tad or -tud

Ends in -umbre

Ends in -d or -z

Note: As you will discover as we go along, there are ALWAYS exceptions in Spanish.

For example, *día* ("day") ends in an -a but is, in fact, masculine. And *lápiz* ("pencil") ends in -z but is masculine as well! And *mamá* is definitely feminine!

Is it a boy... no it's a girl! Oh, it's both!

Here are some more things you should know.

Words that end in -ista are used for both masculine and feminine. For example, *el artista / la artista*, and *el pianista / la pianista*.

Your clue is the article that accompanies the noun.

In bilingual dictionaries, watch out for the (m) or (f) annotations after each noun. This will give you a clue about the gender of the particular word.

It's best to learn the Spanish noun together with the gender. This way, your ears will be more attuned to the sound of the Spanish word and its correct gender.

Noun genders can be overwhelming for language learners. But take it slowly and remember all the rules we shared above. With more and more exposure to the Spanish language, determining the gender will get easier in time.

Spanish Definite Articles

As you may have noticed, the article immediately preceding a noun has to match the gender of the noun. This is different from English, where a simple "the" can suffice in most circumstances.

Take a look at the following articles so you know how to precede your nouns:

Masculine singular - *el*

Masculine plural - *los*

Feminine singular - *la*

Feminine plural - *las*

Workbook Lesson 4: Nouns – Sustantivos

Exercise 1: Say whether the following nouns are masculine or feminine.

1- La periodista: M - F (the journalist)
2- El estudiante: M - F (the student)
3- La piloto: M - F (the pilot)
4- El doctor: M - F (the doctor)
5- La amiga: M - F (the friend)
6- El pintor: M - F (the painter)
7- La juventud: M - F (the youth)

Exercise 2: Classify the following nouns in the table.

Atención, lápiz, mano, vaso, problema, foto, casa, cama, día, cuaderno, cumpleaños, foto, hotel, habitación, libro, página, leche, teatro, noche, lámpara, museo, viernes.

El	La

Exercise 3: Tick the correct answer.

1- ____ casa de Pedro (Pedro's house)
   a. La   b. El   c. Los

2- Ellos compran ____ pastel. (They buy the cake.)
   a. los   b. el   c. la

3- Nosotros no entendemos ____ problema. (We don't understand the problem.)
   a. la   b. el   c. los

4- Abre ____ ventana. (Open the window.)
   a. la   b. los   c. el

5- ¿Dónde está ____ hospital? (Where is the hospital?)
   a. el   b. la   c. los

Exercise 4: Translate the following from English to Spanish.

1- The house
2- The living room
3- The chair
4- The refrigerator
5- The dog

Exercise 5: Translate the following phrases from Spanish to English.

1- La mesa
2- El lápiz
3- El día
4- El libro
5- La comida

Answers:

Exercise 1

1/ La periodista – Fem. 2/ El estudiante – Masc. 3/ La piloto – Fem.
4/ El doctor - Masc. 5/ La amiga - Fem. 6/ El pintor - Masc.
7/ La juventud - Fem.

Exercise 2

EL: el lápiz, el vaso, el problema, el día, el cuaderno, el cumpleaños, el hotel, el libro, el teatro, el museo, el viernes.
LA: la atención, la mano, la foto, la casa, la cama, la foto, la habitación, la página, la leche, la noche, la lámpara.

Exercise 3

1/ La 2/ el 3/ el 4/ la 5/ el

Exercise 4

1/ La casa 2/ La sala 3/ La silla 4/ El refrigerador 5/ El perro

Exercise 5

1/ The table 2/ The pencil 3/ The day 4/ The book 5/ The food

Lesson 5: Numbers – Los números

This lesson is all about numbers! Clearly, they're an important part of any language and are used every day, for talking about dates, times, ages, prices ... the list goes on!

Spanish numbers are either cardinal numbers or ordinal numbers. Cardinal numbers are just numbers. For example "one," "five," "two hundred." Ordinal numbers are similar but used for saying the position or order of something, e.g. "first," "fifth," "two-hundredth."

Pronunciation

There's a pronunciation guide below as hearing the numbers spoken by a native is important to make sure you're saying them more or less right!

Number	Pronunciation
0 = *cero*	SEH-roh

Cardinal Numbers

So, to learn how to count, we need the cardinal numbers.

We're not going to list every number from 0 to 1,000 or 1,000,000 or beyond! Luckily, we have patterns that mean you only have to learn the small numbers (and the big multiples like "hundred" and "thousand") to be able to figure out how to say any number.

Let's start with **0-20**:

Listen to Track 27

0	*Cero* (SEH-roh)
1	*Uno** (OO-noh)
2	*Dos* (dohs)
3	*Tres* (trehs)
4	*Cuatro* (KWAH-troh)
5	*Cinco* (SEEHN-koh)
6	*Seis* (SEH-ees)
7	*Siete* (see-EH-teh)
8	*Ocho* (EH-choh)
9	*Nueve* (noo-EH-beh)

10	*Diez* (dee-EHS)
11	*Once* (OHN-seh)
12	*Doce* (DOH-seh)
13	*Trece* (TREH-seh)
14	*Catorce* (kah-TOHR-seh)
15**	*Quince* (KEEN-seh)
16***	*Dieciséis* (dee-ehs-ee-SEH-ees)
17***	*Diecisiete* (dee-ehs-ee-see-EH-teh)
18***	*Dieciocho* (dee-ehs-ee-OH-choh)
19***	*Diecinueve* (dee-ehs-ee-noo-EH-beh)
20	*Veinte* (BEH-een-teh)

* The number one is *uno*. However, if you want to say that you have one of something, you use *un* for a masculine noun, and *una* for a feminine noun. For example, "*Tengo un hermano y una hermana.*" ("I have one brother and one sister.")

** You may have heard of a celebration called the *quinceañera* that's celebrated in parts of Latin America and parts of the U.S. It marks a girl's 15th birthday and, as you can see, comes from the word *quince* (15) and the word *año* ("year")!

*** The words for 16, 17, 18, and 19 are pretty smart. They come from mashing numbers together. For example, 17 comes from blending together the words *diez y siete* ("ten and seven").

Let's move on to **21-30**:

Listen to Track 28

21*	*Veintiuno* (beh-een-tee-OO-noh)
22	*Veintidós* (beh-een-tee-DOHS)
23	*Veintitrés* (beh-een-tee-TREHS)
24	*Veinticuatro* (beh-een-tee-KWAH-troh)
25	*Veinticinco* (beh-een-tee-SEEHN-koh)
26	*Veintiséis* (beh-een-tee-SEH-ees)
27	*Veintisiete* (beh-een-tee-see-EH-teh)
28	*Veintiocho* (beh-een-tee-OH-choh)
29	*Veintinueve* (beh-een-tee-noo-EH-beh)
30	*Treinta* (TREH-een-tah)

With the twenties, we carry on blending words together, e.g. *veintidós* (22) comes from *veinte y dos* ("twenty and two").

* We mentioned earlier that *uno* becomes *un* or *una* before a noun. It's similar with 21, 31, and so on:

Tú tienes veintiún plátanos. Yo tengo veintiún manzanas. ("You have 21 bananas. I have 21 apples.")

Now, let's look at the **30s**:

Listen to Track 29

31	*Treinta y uno* (treh-een-tah ee OO-noh)
32	*Treinta y dos* (treh-een-tah ee DOHS)
33	*Treinta y tres* (treh-een-tah ee TREHS)
34	*Treinta y cuatro* (treh-een-tah ee KWAH-troh)
35	*Treinta y cinco* (treh-een-tah ee SEEHN-koh)
36	*Treinta y seis* (treh-een-tah ee SEH-ees)
37	*Treinta y siete* (treh-een-tah ee see-EH-teh)
38	*Treinta y ocho* (treh-een-tah ee OH-choh)
39	*Treinta y nueve* (treh-een-tah ee noo-EH-beh)
40	*Cuarenta* (kwah-REHN-tah)

In the thirties, we still do a little bit of math, but we don't need to worry about mashing words together now! For example, 35 is simply *treinta y cinco* ("thirty and five").

The same rule applies for the 40s, 50s, and all the way up through the 90s!

Now that you know that, you just need to get to 100 in multiples of 10, so let's look at **10-100**, to recap the earlier ones and advance up to higher numbers:

Listen to Track 30

10	*Diez* (dee-EHS)
20	*Veinte* (BEH-een-teh)
30	*Treinta* (TREH-een-tah)
40	*Cuarenta* (kwah-REHN-tah)
50	*Cincuenta* (seen-KWEHN-tah)
60	*Sesenta* (seh-SEHN-tah)
70	*Setenta* (seh-TEHN-tah)
80	*Ochenta* (oh-CHEHN-tah)
90	*Noventa* (noh-BEHN-tah)
100	*Ciento* OR cien** (see-EHN-toh) OR (see-EHN)

When you're saying **100**, you can use either *ciento* or *cien,* depending on the context. When we're using it to count a noun, it has to be *cien*.

For example:

Listen to Track 31

| I have a hundred puppies. | *Tengo cien perritos.* |

When we're using numbers from **101-199**, we have to use *ciento:*

102	*Ciento dos* (see-EHN-toh dohs)
132	*Ciento treinta y dos* (see-EHN-toh TREH-een-tah ee dohs)
160	*Ciento sesenta* (see-EHN-toh se-SEHN-tah)

Next, we'll look at the hundreds, from **100-900**.

Listen to Track 32

100	*Ciento* OR *cien* (see-EHN-toh) OR (see-EHN)
200	*Doscientos* (dohs-see-EHN-tohs)
300	*Trescientos* (trehs-see-EHN-tohs)
400	*Cuatrocientos* (kwah-troh-see-EHN-tohs)
500	*Quinientos* (keen-ee-EHN-tohs)
600	*Seiscientos* (seh-ees-see-EHN-tohs)
700	*Setecientos* (seh-teh-see-EHN-tohs)
800	*Ochocientos* (oh-choh-see-EHN-tohs)
900	*Novecientos* (noh-beh-see-EHN-tohs)

Some of them are just counting hundreds, e.g. *cuatrocientos* is a joined-up version of *cuatro cientos*. How many hundreds? Four hundreds. Others (500, 700, and 900) are a tiny bit different – check the spellings.

Now for the big numbers! Let's look at **1,000–1,000,000,000,000**!

Listen to Track 33

1,000*	*Mil* (meel)
10,000	*Diez mil* (dee-ehs MEEL)
100,000	*Cien mil* (see-ehn MEEL)
1,000,000 (a million)	*Un millón* (oon mee-YOHN)
1,000,000,000** (a billion)	*Mil millones* (meel mee-YOH-ness)
1,000,000,000,000 (a trillion)	*Un billón* (oon bee-YOHN)

*In Spanish numbers, commas and decimal points are used the same as in English. To separate numbers higher than four digits, a comma is acceptable, but a space is also commonly used (2,000 or 2 000).

In Spanish, one billion does **not translate to *un billón*. Instead, *mil millones* (one thousand millions) is used to refer to the English billion. *Un billón* refers to a million millions, which is known as one trillion in English.

How to say your age

In English, we use the verb "to be" when it comes to age. In Spanish, we use "to have."

The word for "year(s)" is *año(s)*. That little squiggle on the *ñ* is super important. If you skip it, you're talking about how many anuses you have. You have been warned!

Listen to Track 34

| I am 21 years old. | *Tengo veintiún años* OR *Tengo veintiuno.* |
| María is 69 years old. | *María tiene sesenta y nueve años.* |

Ordinal Numbers

As we mentioned at the start, ordinal numbers are used for stating the position or order of something.

First of all, let's look at **1st–20th**:

Listen to Track 35

First	*Primero* OR *primer** (pree-MEH-roh) OR (pree-MEHR)
Second	*Segundo* (seh-'goon-doh)
Third	*Tercero* OR *tercer** (tehr-SEH-roh) OR (tehr-SEHR)
Fourth	*Cuarto* (KWAHR-toh)
Fifth	*Quinto* (KEEN-toh)
Sixth	*Sexto* (SEHKS-toh)
Seventh	*Séptimo* (SEHP-tee-moh)
Eighth	*Octavo* (oc-TAH-boh)
Ninth	*Noveno* (noh-BEH-noh)
Tenth	*Décimo* (DEH-see-moh)

* *primero* becomes *primer* before a masculine singular noun, and *tercero* becomes *tercer*.

Note that the Spanish ordinals all end in -*o*, which is simpler than English (we have "-st" and "-nd" and "-rd" and "-th" to choose from!).

Instead of writing out whole words, in English we use those last letters with the figure. We do the same in Spanish. The last letter is always either *o* for a masculine noun, or *a* if it's a feminine noun.

1st	1º
2nd	2º
3rd time	3ª vez

Workbook Lesson 5: Numbers – Los números

Exercise 1: Write the number as a figure.

1- Veintitrés - _____
2- Ciento noventa - _____
3- Cero - _____
4- Cuarenta - _____
5- Treinta y siete - _____

Exercise 2: Complete the exercise by adding the numbers.

1- Duermo _____ horas al día. (I sleep eight hours a day.)
2- Él va al gimnasio _____ días a la semana. (He goes to the gym two days a week.)
3- Ellos van al cine _____ veces al mes. (They go to the movies three times a month.)
4- Camila estudia español _____ horas a la semana. (Camila studies Spanish seven hours a week.)
5- Pedro va de compras _____ veces al mes. (Pedro goes shopping three times a month.)

Exercise 3: Write the following numbers in words.

1- 15 de diciembre
2- 45 kilómetros
3- 11 alumnos
4- 51 kilos
5- 61 semanas

Exercise 4: Write the phone numbers, as shown in the example.

Example: Sara 977389583 - nueve siete siete tres ocho nueve cinco ocho tres

1- Nick 9758328457 - _____
2- Pedro 9874338384 - _____
3- Pierre 31287384861 - _____
4- Camila 9872743338 - _____
5- Andrés 9384559285 - _____

Exercise 5: Complete the sentences with the ordinal numbers shown in the English version.

1- Pedro vive en el _____ piso. (Pedro lives on the fifth floor.)
2- Las oficinas de IKEA están en el _____ piso. (IKEA's offices are on the third floor.)
3- La oficina está en la _____ planta. (The office is on the eighth floor.)
4- La academia Cervantes está en la _____ planta. (The Cervantes Academy is on the second floor.)
5- Hay un despacho de abogados en el _____ piso. (There is a law firm on the seventh floor.)

Exercise 6: Write the numbers that appear in brackets.

1- Valencia es el (1°) _____ en la liga. (Valencia is the first in the league.)
2- La D es la letra (4°) _____ del alfabeto. (D is the fourth letter of the alphabet.)
3- Camila y María acabaron (5°) _____ en el campeonato de tenis. (Camila and María finished fifth in the Tennis Championship.)
4- Andrés es el (3°) _____ de sus hermanos. (Javi is the third of his brothers.)
5- Febrero es el (2°) _____ mes del año. (February is the second month of the year.)

Answers:

Exercise 1

1/ 23 2/ 190 3/ 0 4/ 40 5/ 37

Exercise 2

1/ Duermo ocho horas al día. 2/ Él va al gimnasio dos días a la semana. 3/ Ellos van al cine tres veces al mes. 4/ Camila estudia español siete horas a la semana. 5/ Pedro va de compras tres veces al mes.

Exercise 3

1/ Quince de diciembre. 2/ Cuarenta y cinco kilómetros. 3/Once alumnos. 4/Cincuenta y un kilos. 5/Sesenta y un semanas.

Exercise 4

1/ Nueve siete cinco ocho tres dos ocho cuatro cinco siete. 2/Nueve ocho siete cuatro tres tres ocho tres ocho cuatro. 3/Tres uno dos ocho siete tres ocho cuatro ocho seis uno. 4/Nueve ocho siete dos siete cuatro tres tres tres ocho. 5/Nueve tres ocho cuatro cinco cinco nueve dos ocho cinco

Exercise 5

1/quinto 2/ tercer 3/ octava 4/ segunda 5/ séptimo

Exercise 6

1/ primero 2/ cuarta 3/ quintas 4/ tercero 5/segundo

Lesson 6: Verb conjugations – Conjugaciones verbales

Spanish verb conjugations are much more comprehensive than English verb conjugations. Although English conjugates as well, these conjugations are usually very simple, such as "I play" and "he plays."

Verb conjugations consist of changing the form of a verb to show the tense, and to match the number and person of the subject. A conjugated verb will include a lot of information about who is doing the action, when they're doing it, and how many people are doing it.

There are two main types of verbs in Spanish when it comes to conjugations: regular verbs and irregular verbs. The good news is that conjugating regular verbs is very predictable. The bad news is that conjugating irregular verbs is ... not. We'll cover both of them in this lesson to get you conjugating your verbs right away!

Regular Verbs

All regular verbs in the infinitive form end in **-ar**, **-er**, or **-ir**. This makes them very easy to identify and even easier to conjugate! The first thing you need to do is identify the verb stem and the infinitive ending. For example:

Listen to Track 36

- Saltar = salt + **ar**
- Comer = com + **er**
- Vivir = viv + **ir**

Once you've identified which verb type you're dealing with and what the verb stem and infinitive ending are, you can start conjugating!

Conjugating -ar verbs

To conjugate an -ar verb, you will first have to drop the infinitive ending and use the corresponding ending. Let's take a look at the conjugation of the verb *saltar* (to jump):

Verb stem: salt

Infinitive ending: -ar

Listen to Track 37

Yo salt**o**	Nosotros salt**amos**
Tú salt**as**	Ustedes salt**an**
Él/ella/usted salt**a**	Ellos/ellas salt**an**

As you can see, all you need to do is drop the infinitive ending and replace it with one of these endings!

Let's take a look at a couple other examples:

Listen to Track 38

Caminar (to walk):

Verb stem: *camin*

Infinitive ending: *-ar*

Yo camin**o**	Nosotros camin**amos**
Tú camin**as**	Ustedes camin**an**
Él/ella/usted camin**a**	Ellos/ellas camin**an**

Listen to Track 39

Bailar (to dance):

Verb stem: *bail*

Infinitive ending: *-ar*

Yo bail**o**	Nosotros bail**amos**
Tú bail**as**	Ustedes bail**an**
Él/ella/usted bail**a**	Ellos/ellas bail**an**

Conjugating -er verbs

Another very popular verb ending is -er. These verbs are conjugated very similarly to the -ar verbs, although the endings are a little different. Let's take a look at the verb *comer* (to eat):

Verb stem: *com*

Infinitive ending: *-er*

Listen to Track 40

Yo com**o**	Nosotros com**emos**
Tú com**es**	Ustedes com**en**
Él/ella/usted com**e**	Ellos/ellas com**en**

Pretty simple, right! With a little bit of studying and some practice, you'll be able to master the verb conjugations expertly. Let's take a look at some more examples:

Listen to Track 41

Leer (to read):

Verb stem: *le*

Infinitive ending: *-er*

Yo le**o**	Nosotros le**emos**
Tú le**es**	Ustedes le**en**
Él/ella/usted le**e**	Ellos/ellas le**en**

Listen to Track 42

Beber (to drink):

Verb stem: *beb*

Infinitive ending: *-er*

Yo beb**o**	Nosotros beb**emos**
Tú beb**es**	Ustedes beb**en**
Él/ella/usted beb**e**	Ellos/ellas beb**en**

Conjugating -ir verbs

Finally, we have the -ir verbs. These are pretty easy to conjugate, just like the other two kinds of regular verbs. Just replace the infinitive ending with the ending corresponding to the person and number of the subject. Let's take a look at the verb *vivir (to live)*:

Verb stem: *viv*

Infinitive ending: *-ir*

Listen to Track 43

Yo vivo	*Nosotros vivimos*
Tú vives	*Ustedes viven*
Él/ella/usted vive	*Ellos/ellas viven*

Note that the verb endings are almost identical to the endings of -er verbs, except for the first person plural, where the ending is **-imos** instead of **-emos**.

Here are a couple of other examples.

Listen to Track 44

Abrir (to open):

Verb stem: *abr*

Infinitive ending: *-ir*

Yo abro	*Nosotros abrimos*
Tú abres	*Ustedes abren*
Él/ella/usted abre	*Ellos/ellas abren*

Listen to Track 45

Escribir (to write):

Verb stem: *escrib*

Infinitive ending: *-ir*

Yo escribo	*Nosotros escribimos*
Tú escribes	*Ustedes escriben*
Él/ella/usted escribe	*Ellos/ellas escriben*

Irregular Verbs

Irregular verbs are slightly more complex than regular verbs. In Spanish, a verb is considered irregular when there is a change in the verb stem in addition to the ending. This means that you can't use a plug-and-play strategy like with regular verbs. Instead, you will have to spend some time memorizing the different conjugations.

Luckily, there aren't that many irregular verbs and, with enough exposure and practice, you will memorize all the conjugations fairly quickly. Try to be patient with your progress! You'll nail the conjugations in time.

With that said, there are some patterns in irregular verbs that you'll be able to follow. Let's take a look at a few:

Verb ending in -ar – Stem change of e→ie

Irregular verbs ending in -er may have a stem change where the **e** has to be replaced with an **ie**. This stem change replacement does not apply to the first person plural, so you can continue using the regular verb stem. The endings are still the same as regular verbs. Let's look at a couple of examples:

Listen to Track 46

Cerrar (to close):

Verb stem: *cerr*

Infinitive ending: *-ar*

Verb stem after change: *cierr*

Yo cierr**o**	Nosotros cerr**amos**
Tú cierr**as**	Ustedes cierr**an**
Él/ella/usted cierr**a**	Ellos/ellas cierr**an**

Listen to Track 47

Pensar (to think):

Verb stem: *pens*

Infinitive ending: *-ar*

Verb stem after change: *piens*

Yo piens**o**	Nosotros pens**amos**
Tú piens**as**	Ustedes piens**an**
Él/ella/usted piens**a**	Ellos/ellas piens**an**

Verb ending in -ar – Stem change of o→u

Another possible verb stem change for verbs ending in -ar is a change from **o** to **u**. These verb stem changes also do not apply to the first person plural. Let's review a couple of examples:

Listen to Track 48

Encontrar (to find):

Verb stem: *encontr*

Infinitive ending: *-ar*

Verb stem after change: *enc**u**entr*

Yo encuentr**o**	Nosotros encontr**amos**
Tú encuentr**as**	Ustedes encuentr**an**
Él/ella/usted encuentr**a**	Ellos/ellas encuentr**an**

Listen to Track 49

Recordar (to remember):

Verb stem: *record*

Infinitive ending: *-ar*

Verb stem after change: *rec**u**erd*

Yo recuerd**o**	Nosotros record**amos**
Tú recuerd**as**	Ustedes recuerd**an**
Él/ella/usted recuerd**a**	Ellos/ellas recuerd**an**

Verb ending in -er – Stem change of e→ie

Just like -ar verbs, you can expect a stem change of **e** to **ie** with -er verbs. Again, these do not apply to first person plural, so continue using the regular verb for those!

Listen to Track 50

Entender (to understand):

Verb stem: *entend*

Infinitive ending: *-er*

Verb stem after change: *entiend*

Yo entien**do**	Nosotros entend**emos**
Tú entien**des**	Ustedes entien**den**
Él/ella/usted entien**de**	Ellos/ellas entien**den**

Listen to Track 51

Querer (to want):

Verb stem: *quer*

Infinitive ending: *-er*

Verb stem after change: *quier*

Yo quier**o**	Nosotros quer**emos**
Tú quier**es**	Ustedes quier**en**
Él/ella/usted quier**e**	Ellos/ellas quier**en**

Verb ending in -er – Stem change of u→ue

Another possible verb stem change for irregular verbs ending in -er is a change from **u** to **ue**. Once again, ignore the verb stem change if you're conjugating in the first person plural!

Listen to Track 52

Poder (to be able to):

Verb stem: *pod*

Infinitive ending: *-er*

Verb stem after change: *pued*

Yo pued**o**	Nosotros pod**emos**
Tú pued**es**	Ustedes pued**en**
Él/ella/usted pued**e**	Ellos/ellas pued**en**

Listen to Track 53

Volver (to return):

Verb stem: *volv*

Infinitive ending: *-er*

Verb stem after change: *v**ue**lv*

Yo vuelv**o**	Nosotros volv**emos**
Tú vuelv**es**	Ustedes vuelv**en**
Él/ella/usted vuelv**e**	Ellos/ellas vuelv**en**

Verb ending in -ir – Stem change of e→ie

Finally, we have the -ir verbs. These irregular verbs can have up to three different stem changes. The first one we'll cover is the change from **e** to **ie**. Let's take a look at a couple of examples:

Listen to Track 54

Mentir (to lie):

Verb stem: *ment*

Infinitive ending: *-ir*

Verb stem after change: *mient*

Yo mient**o**	Nosotros mentimos
Tú mient**es**	Ustedes mient**en**
Él/ella/usted mient**e**	Ellos/ellas mient**en**

Listen to Track 55

Preferir (to prefer):

Verb stem: *prefer*

Infinitive ending: *-ir*

Verb stem after change: *pref**ie**r*

Yo prefier**o**	Nosotros prefer**imos**
Tú prefier**es**	Ustedes prefier**en**
Él/ella/usted prefier**e**	Ellos/ellas prefier**en**

Verb ending in -ir – Stem change of o→ue

The next verb stem change is one you're already familiar with: from **o** to **ue**. Irregular verbs ending in -ir can also experience this kind of verb stem change. These types of verbs aren't as common, so let's take a look at one example:

Listen to Track 56

Dormir (to sleep):

Verb stem: *dorm*

Infinitive ending: *-ir*

Verb stem after change: *d**ue**rm*

Yo duerm**o**	Nosotros dorm**imos**
Tú duerm**es**	Ustedes duerm**en**
Él/ella/usted duerm**e**	Ellos/ellas duerm**en**

Verb ending in -ir – Stem change of e→i

Finally, we have a stem change from **e** to **i** in irregular verbs ending in -ir. This is a very common type of verb stem change, especially as -ir is one of the most common verb endings. Let's take a look at a couple of examples:

Listen to Track 57

Pedir (to ask for):

Verb stem: *ped*

Infinitive ending: *-ir*

Verb stem after change: *pid*

Yo pid**o**	Nosotros ped**imos**
Tú pid**es**	Ustedes pid**en**
Él/ella/usted pid**e**	Ellos/ellas pid**en**

Listen to Track 58

Repetir (to repeat):

Verb stem: *repet*

Infinitive ending: *-ir*

Verb stem after change: *rep**i**t*

*Yo repit**o***	*Nosotros repetimos*
*Tú repit**es***	*Ustedes repit**en***
*Él/ella/usted repit**e***	*Ellos/ellas repit**en***

Null-Subject Language

Spanish is what we call a "null-subject language."

This means that, due to the variety of verb endings, we can leave out the subject of the verb and it still makes sense. Take the verb *vender* ("sell") as an example. In English, most of the verb endings are the same:

I	sell	We	sell
You	sell	You (plural)	sell
He/she/it	sells	They	sell

So if you were to say "sell houses" you'd have no idea who is doing the selling. For that reason, in English we have to include the subject to differentiate between "I sell houses," "you sell houses," "we sell houses," and "they sell houses."

In Spanish, each subject in each tense pretty much has its own verb ending. So if I say "*vendo* casas," it's perfectly clear that *I'm* selling the houses, because of the 'o' at the end. There's no need to say "*yo vendo casas*."

Examples

Take a look at these examples, and try to spot how the verb endings often allow us to drop the subject:

- **-ar verbs**

Listen to Track 59

~~Yo~~ habl**o**.	I speak.
¿Por qué ~~tú~~ me mir**as**?	Why are you looking at me?
Carolina bail**a** bien.*	Carolina dances well.
~~Nosotros~~ nad**amos** en el mar.	We swim in the sea.
¿~~Ustedes~~ trabaj**an** por aquí?	Do you (plural) work around here?
~~Ellas~~ tom**an** riesgos.	They take risks.

*Examples like this are a little more complicated. The verb ending -*a* could refer to he, she or it, or you (formal), so it may be necessary to include the subject to clarify who exactly we are talking about. But don't forget the power of context. If we were reading a book all about Camila the ballerina then we wouldn't need to say "Camila es bailarina de ballet. Camila baila bien. Camila tiene 30 años." It would be clear that we were talking about Camila, so we could drop her name and just say: "Camila es bailarina de ballet. Baila bien. Tiene 30 años."

Workbook Lesson 6: Verb conjugations – Conjugaciones verbales

Exercise 1: Conjugate the following verbs according to the person and number.

Comer:

Yo _____	Nosotros _____
Tú _____	Ustedes _____
Él/ella/usted _____	Ellos/ellas _____

Escribir:

Yo _____	Nosotros _____
Tú _____	Ustedes _____
Él/ella/usted _____	Ellos/ellas _____

Encontrar:

Yo _____	Nosotros _____
Tú _____	Ustedes _____
Él/ella/usted _____	Ellos/ellas _____

Exercise 2: Complete the sentence with the correct conjugation.

1. Yo _____ (poder) escribir un libro.
2. Creo que ellos _____ (mentir) mucho.
3. Nosotros _____ (querer) ir a la playa.
4. Seguramente ella lo _____ (encontrar).
5. ¿Qué _____ (pensar) ustedes?

Exercise 3: Identify whether the following verbs are regular or irregular.

1. Mentir _____
2. Volver _____
3. Cerrar _____
4. Beber _____
5. Caminar _____

Exercise 4: Translate the following sentences into Spanish.

1- Do you remember her name?

2- They won't come back until Monday.

3- He wants pasta.

4- We don't understand English.

5- I don't quite remember his name.

Answers:

Exercise 1

1/ Yo como, tú comes, él/ella/usted come, nosotros comemos, ustedes comen, ellos/ellas comen 2/ Yo escribo, tú escribes, él/ella/usted escribe, nosotros escribimos, ustedes escriben, ellos/ellas escriben 3/ Yo encuentro, tú encuentras, él/ella/ustedes encuentran, nosotros encontramos, ustedes encuentran, ellos/ellas encuentran

Exercise 2

1/ Yo puedo escribir un libro. 2/ Creo que ellos mienten mucho.
3/ Nosotros queremos ir a la playa. 4/ Seguramente ella lo encuentra.
5/¿Qué piensan ustedes?

Exercise 3

1/ Irregular 2/ Irregular 3/ Irregular 4/ Regular 5/ Regular

Exercise 4

1/ ¿Recuerdas cómo se llamaba? 2/ Ellos no vuelven hasta el lunes.
3/ Él quiere pasta. 4/ Nosotros no entendemos inglés.
5/No recuerdo bien su nombre.

Lesson 7: "There is"/"There are" – Hay

In this lesson, we'll look at how to say "there is" and "there are" in Spanish. It's simpler than you might think!

Two Forms of *Haber*:

The verb we're going to need is the verb *haber*, which roughly translates as "to have/to be."

There are two ways to use it. The first one is by conjugating it like this:

Listen to Track 60

Yo he	Nosotros hemos
Tú has	Ustedes han
Él/ella/usted ha	Ellos/ellas han

The second way is when we want to use *haber* to denote that something exists, i.e. to say "there is" or "there are." To do this, we only ever need the third person singular, but instead of using *ha*, we use *hay* (but don't ask why we add the "y"!).

For example:

Hay pan en la cocina.	There is bread in the kitchen.

Hay is so useful in Spanish, so it's worth knowing how it's pronounced. It's not like "hay," the stuff that horses eat. It's more like "ay ay ay!"

Singular and Plural

Hay is useful because it's the same whether you're saying "there is one thing" (singular) or "there are multiple things" (plural)! This is the only form you need in the present tense.

We do need to change this in different tenses but again, there's only one form for both singular and plural.

How *hay* can be used

Haber can be used in pretty much every tense you can think of.

Let's check out some examples.

Present

Listen to Track 61

As we've seen, the word to use is *hay*.

¿*Hay* algún lugar aquí que venda fruta?	Is there any place here that sells fruit?
Hay lugares hermosos en Colombia.	There are beautiful places in Colombia.

Preterite

Listen to Track 62

To use it in the preterite, which is a past tense, we need to say *hubo*. Use this verb conjugation anytime you want to talk about something that happened in the past but is no longer happening. The English equivalent of this is "there was/were."

Hubo una reunión esta mañana.	There was a meeting this morning.
Hubo muchos problemas durante la reunión.	There were lots of problems during the meeting.

Imperfect

Listen to Track 63

The imperfect (another past tense) version is *había*. This is the equivalent of "was/were." Use this verb conjugation when you want to describe something that happened or existed in the past for a while, but no longer exists.

Pasé una hora buscando, pero no *había* nadie en el edificio.	I spent an hour searching but there was nobody in the building.
Vi que *había* dos computadoras libres en la biblioteca.	I saw that there were two free computers in the library.

Future

Listen to Track 64

For the future tense, the verb is *habrá*.

Habrá mucha gente en la fiesta.	There will be lots of people at the party.
Alicia, *habrá* dos chicos en el departamento cuando regreses del trabajo. No te asustes, son amigos míos.	Alicia, there will be two guys in the apartment when you get home from work. Don't be scared, they're friends of mine.

Future (*ir a ...*)

The other way of forming future phrases (especially for the near future) uses *ir a* + infinitive, so here we use *ir a* + *hab er*. *Ir* will be in the present tense third person singular (*va*), and *haber* stays in the infinitive. This is the equivalent of the English "there will be."

Listen to Track 65

| Va a haber otro restaurante en la avenida principal. | There will be another restaurant on the main avenue. |
| Va a haber 500 vasos y botellas de agua para los participantes de la carrera. | There will be 500 cups and bottles of water for the participants of the race. |

Perfect

Listen to Track 66

The perfect tense describes something that either occurred at an undefined time in the past or an action that started in the past and has continued into the present. The English equivalent for this is "there has been."

Don't get confused here, just follow this formula: *haber* + *habido*.

The formula is always *ha* + *habido*.

¿Qué ha pasado aquí?	What's happened here?
Ha habido* una pelea.	There's been a fight.
Ha habido varias denuncias contra el jefe.	There have been several complaints made against the manager.

*Although the perfect tense is correct (in Spanish *Pretérito Perfecto*), it is not commonly used in day-to-day communication **in Mexico**. Instead, the simple past is used. (¿Que **pasó** aquí? – **Hubo** una pelea).

Workbook Lesson 7: "There is"/"There are" – Hay

Exercise 1: Create sentences similar to the example below.

Example: Las flores/El jardín. En el jardín, hay flores (In the garden, there are flowers.)

1- Las nubes/el cielo. (clouds/sky)

2- Los estudiantes/la escuela. (pupils/school)

3- Los juguetes/el cuarto del niño. (toys/the kid's room)

4- Las mesas/el salón. (tables/classroom)

5- La ropa/la lavadora. (clothes/washing machine)

Exercise 2: Create past sentences using "hay" (see the example below).

Example: Hay un perro. → Había un perro. (There was a dog.)

1- Hay un concierto. (There was a concert.)

2- Hay aire acondicionado en la habitación. (There was air conditioning in the room.)

3- Hay un balcón en el departamento. (There was a balcony in this apartment.)

4- Hay un banco cerca de aquí. (There was a bank near here.)

5- Hay taxis aquí. (There were taxis here.)

Exercise 3: What is in your room? Imagine you are in your room and create sentences like the example.

Example: un espejo. *Hay un espejo.* (There's a mirror.) – *No hay espejo.* (There's no mirror.)

1- una mesa (a table)

2- una lámpara (a lamp)

3- una televisión (a TV)

4- un reloj (a clock)

5- un sofá (a sofa)

Exercise 4: Transform these negative sentences into past sentences using "hay".

1- En mi colonia no hay metro. (There is no metro in my neighborhood.)

2- ¿No hay una cafetería por aquí? (Isn't there a coffee shop around here?)

3- En Guadalajara no hay muchos museos. (There aren't many museums in Guadalajara.)

4- No hay diez alumnos en mi clase. (There aren't ten students in my class.)

5- En mi casa no hay dos albercas. (There aren't two pools in my house.)

Exercise 5: Re-order these words to create sentences that make sense.

1- para ti / un paquete/ hay
2- para comer / hay / algo
3- ratón / en / un/ mi / habitación/ hay
4- en mi calle / un hotel / hay
5- algo / hay /en mi sopa

Answers:

Exercise 1

1/ Hay nubes en el cielo. 2/ Hay estudiantes en la escuela. 3/ Hay juguetes en el cuarto del niño. 4/ Hay mesas en el salón. 5/ Hay ropa en la lavadora.

Exercise 2

1/ Había un concierto. 2/ Había aire acondicionado en la habitación. 3/ Había un balcón en el departamento. 4/ Había un banco cerca de aquí. 5/ Había taxis aquí.

Exercise 3

1/ No hay una mesa. 2/ Hay una lámpara. 3/ Hay una televisión. 4/ No hay un reloj.

5/ Hay un sofá.

Exercise 4

1/ En mi colonia había metro. 2/ Había una cafetería por aquí. 3/ En Guadalajara había muchos museos. 4/ Había diez alumnos en mi clase. 5/ En mi casa había dos albercas.

Exercise 5

1/ Hay un paquete para ti. 2/ Hay algo para comer. 3/ Hay un ratón en mi habitación. 4/ En mi calle hay un hotel. 5/ Hay algo en mi sopa.

Lesson 8: Present tense – El presente simple

The Present

Talking about the present in Spanish is pretty easy. The hardest part is simply familiarizing yourself with the conjugations themselves.

The present tense in Spanish is very versatile. It can be used to talk about the permanent facts and routines, a continuous action taking place in the present, and the future.

Listen to Track 67

Estudio español. (I study Spanish.)

Leo el libro. (I am reading the book.)

Luego te llamo. (I'll call you then.)

There is, however, a Spanish equivalent to the English present progressive that can be used to talk about something going on at the current moment. It is very useful to be familiar with it, and it will help you a lot when speaking to a native Spanish speaker!

The Present Progressive

The present progressive is, like in English, saying "to be doing X."

It is formed using the verb *estar* and has the following construction:

Estar + present participle (in English, the verb ending in -ing)

The conjugation of the verb *estar* is:

Listen to Track 68

Yo estoy

Tú estás

Él/Ella/Usted está

Nosotros estamos

Ustedes están

Ellos/Ellas están

The present participle ending in Spanish is pretty simple to learn. With -*ar* verbs, you will simply remove the ending and add -*ando*. With -*er*/-*ir* verbs, you will do the same, but add the ending -*iendo*.

Listen to Track 69

-ar	-er/-ir
Hablar- hablando	*Comer- comiendo*
Estudiar- estudiando	*Vivir- viviendo*
Andar- andando	*Hacer- haciendo*

If you have a stem-changing verb, you will change the appropriate vowel, and add the ending.

e:i	o:u
Decir- diciendo	*Dormir- durmiendo*
Servir- sirviendo	*Poder- pudiendo*

And, there are some instances when the spelling needs to change so as not to change the pronunciation:

Listen to Track 70

Caer- Cayendo

Leer- Leyendo

Ir- Yendo

Creer- Creyendo

Some examples of using this construction to talk about events taking place in the present are:

Listen to Track 71

First person singular: *Estoy hablando con mi madre.* (I am talking to my mom.)

Second person singular: *Estás yendo muy despacio.* (You're going very slowly.)

Third person singular: *Está estudiando biología.* (He/she is studying biology.)

First person plural: *Estamos viviendo en Guadalajara.* (We are living in Guadalajara.)

Second person plural: *Están viendo la tele.* (You [plural] are watching TV.)

Third person plural: *Están durmiendo.* (They are sleeping.)

The constructions mentioned above are all commonly used in everyday speech, and are simple, easy-to-remember ways of talking about the ongoing present.

Now that you know a bit of Spanish vocabulary, let's use it in some sentences.

Helpful verbs in present tense

Quite a few verbs in Spanish are irregular, meaning they don't follow these patterns. It's important to learn the most common ones, as they're often some of the most useful verbs in the language for speaking in present tense.

Listen to Track 72

- *ir* (to go)

Yo voy	Nosotros vamos
Tú vas	Ustedes van
Él/ella va	Ellos/ellas van

Examples:

Voy al mercado.	I'm going to the market.
Pedro va al gimnasio.	Pedro goes to the gym.
Vamos a la playa.	We are going to the beach.

Listen to Track 73

- *hacer* (to do/to make)

Yo hago	Nosotros hacemos
Tú haces	Ustedes hacen
Él/ella hace	Ellos/ellas hacen

Examples:

Los martes, hago el súper.	On Tuesdays, I do the grocery shopping.
¿Qué haces?	What are you doing?
Hacen mucho ruido.	They're making a lot of noise.

Listen to Track 74

- **ser (to be)***

Yo soy	Nosotros somos
Tú eres	Ustedes son
Él/ella es	Ellos/ellas son

Examples:

Eres hermosa.	You are beautiful.
Son idiotas.	You are idiots.
Son hombres.	They are men.

Listen to Track 75

- **estar (to be)***

Yo estoy	Nosotros estamos
Tú estás	Ustedes están
Él/ella está	Ellos/ellas están

Examples:

¿Dónde está la biblioteca?	Where is the library?
Están en mi casa.	You (plural) are in my house.
¿Señores, cómo están?	Gentlemen, how are you?

*The differences between these two versions of "to be" can be quite subtle and take a while to learn. Just remember for now that there are two verbs that mean "to be." We will learn more on the distinction between *ser* and *estar* in Lesson 9.

Listen to Track 76

- **haber (to have)***

Yo he	Nosotros hemos
Tú has	Ustedes han
Él/ella ha/hay	Ellos/ellas han

*This verb is usually used in compound tenses.

Another use of *haber* is that the third person singular form *hay* is used to mean "there is/there are."

He terminado.	I have finished.
Pedro ha escrito algo.	Pedro has written something.
Hay un ratón en la casa.	There is a mouse in the house.

Listen to Track 77

- ***tener*** **(to have)**

Yo tengo	Nosotros tenemos
Tú tienes	Ustedes tienen
Él/ella tiene	Ellos/ellas tienen

Examples:

Sara tiene fiebre.	Sara has a fever.
Tenemos muchos problemas.	We have a lot of problems.
Los perros tienen muchos juguetes.	The dogs have lots of toys.

Listen to Track 78

- ***poner*** **(to put)**

Yo pongo	Nosotros ponemos
Tú pones	Ustedes ponen
Él/ella pone	Ellos/ellas ponen

Examples:

¿Te pongo más ensalada?	Shall I give you more salad?
¿Por qué pones tus cosas en mi habitación?	Why are you putting your things in my room?
La radio pone mis canciones favoritas.	The radio puts on my favorite songs.

Listen to Track 79

- **decir** (to say)

Yo digo	Nosotros decimos
Tú dices	Ustedes dicen
Él/ella dice	Ellos/ellas dicen

Examples:

Digo la verdad.	I'm telling the truth.
A veces mi padre dice groserías.	Sometimes my dad swears.
Dicen que todo pasa por alguna razón.	They say that everything happens for a reason.

Listen to Track 80

- **ver** (to see)

Yo veo	Nosotros vemos
Tú ves	Ustedes ven
Él/ella ve	Ellos/ellas ven

Examples:

Ya me has hecho daño, ¿ves?	Now you've hurt me, see?
Ven demasiadas películas.	You watch too many films.
Tus profesores lo ven todo.	Your teachers see everything.

Listen to Track 81

- **saber** (to know something/to taste)

Yo sé	Nosotros sabemos
Tú sabes	Ustedes saben
Él/ella sabe	Ellos/ellas saben

Examples:

No lo sé.	I don't know.
El helado sabe a vainilla.	The ice cream tastes of vanilla.
Sabemos cantar.	We know how to sing.

Listen to Track 82

- **venir** (to come)

Yo vengo	Nosotros venimos
Tú vienes	Ustedes vienen
Él/ella viene	Ellos/ellas vienen

Examples:

Ya vengo.	I'm coming.
¿Señora, viene a la reunión?	Madame, are you coming to the meeting?
Vienen a la fiesta.	They are coming to the party.

Listen to Track 83

- **conocer** (to know someone)

Yo conozco	Nosotros conocemos
Tú conoces	Ustedes conocen
Él/ella conoce	Ellos/ellas conocen

Examples:

Conozco a Andrés.	I know Andrés.
¿Ustedes se conocen?	Do you know each other?
Conocen a Shakira.	They know Shakira.

Listen to Track 84

- **dar** (to give)

Yo doy	Nosotros damos
Tú das	Ustedes dan
Él/ella da	Ellos/ellas dan

Examples:

Doy mis consejos.	I give my advice.
¿Me das tu número de teléfono?	Will you give me your number?
Estamos dando pasos para mejorar la situación.	We are taking steps to improve the situation.

Listen to Track 85

- **salir (to go out)**

Yo salgo	Nosotros salimos
Tú sales	Ustedes salen
Él/ella sale	Ellos/ellas salen

Examples:

Salgo cada viernes.	I go out every Friday.
Sale más barato así.	It works out cheaper this way.
Normalmente salen por esa puerta.	Normally they go out through that door.

Listen to Track 86

- **poder (to be able to)**

o → ue

puedo	podemos
puedes	pueden
puede	pueden

Examples:

No puedo ir.	I can't go.
¿Pueden venir?	Can you (plural) come?
Puede entrar.	You (formal) may enter.

Listen to Track 87

- **volver (to return)**

o → ue

vuelvo	volvemos
vuelves	vuelven
vuelve	vuelven

Examples:

Los lunes vuelvo a casa a medianoche.	On Mondays I return home at midnight.
Sandra siempre vuelve con su ex.	Sandra always goes back to her ex.
¿Chicas, a qué hora vuelven?	Girls, what time are you coming back?

Listen to Track 88

- ***empezar* (to start)**

e → ie

empiezo	empezamos
empiezas	empiezan
empieza	empiezan

Examples:

La película empieza pronto.	The movie starts soon.
Cuando estamos arregladas, nos dan ganas de salir	When we're dressed up, we feel like going out.
Las canciones empiezan bien.	The songs start well.

Listen to Track 89

- ***pensar* (to think)**

e → ie

pienso	pensamos
piensas	piensan
piensa	piensan

Examples:

¿Piensas en mí?	Do you think about me?
Tu madre y yo pensamos que eres muy inteligente.	Your mother and I think that you're very intelligent.
Ana y María piensan en rentar el departamento.	Ana and María are thinking about renting the apartment.

Listen to Track 90

- *preferir* (to prefer)

e → ie

prefiero	*preferimos*
prefieres	*prefieren*
prefiere	*prefieren*

Examples:

Prefiero vivir en Alemania.	I prefer living in Germany.
¿Cuál prefiere usted?	Which one do you (formal) prefer?
¿Prefieren pastel o helado?	Do you (plural) prefer cake or ice cream?

Listen to Track 91

- *repetir* (to repeat)

e → i

repito	*repetimos*
repites	*repiten*
repite	*repiten*

Examples:

Repito: no vas a la fiesta.	I say again: you are not going to the party.
A veces cenamos y luego repetimos.	Sometimes we have dinner then have second helpings.
Repiten los mismos errores.	They make the same mistakes.

Listen to Track 92

- ***pedir* (to ask for)**

e → i

pido	pedimos
pides	piden
pide	piden

Examples:

No pido nada de él.	I'm not asking him for anything.
El gato pide leche.	The cat asks for milk.
Piden voluntarios.	They are looking for volunteers.

Good job!

That's a lot of example sentences to get through, so well done! Start by learning the regular verb endings, practice a little every day, then think about moving onto the irregular ones!

Workbook Lesson 8: Present tense – El presente simple

Exercise 1: Conjugate the verbs between brackets in the simple present tense.

1- Yo (amar) _____ mucho esta película. (I really like this movie.)
2- Ellos (trabajar) _____ día y noche. (They work day and night.)
3- Ella (habla) _____ muy bien español. (She speaks Spanish very well.)
4- Nosotros (comer) _____ fuera esta noche. (We are eating out tonight.)
5- ¿Usted (pagar) _____ en efectivo o con tarjeta de crédito? (Are you going to pay in cash or by credit card?)

Exercise 2: Conjugate the verbs between brackets in the simple present tense.

1- Nosotros (esperar) _____ el resultado desde la mañana. (We've been waiting for the results since this morning.)
2- ¿Qué ruta (tomar) _____ para ir al súper? (Which road do I take to go to the supermarket?)
3- Ellos (vender) _____ ropa bonita. (They sell beautiful clothes.)
4- Ella (responder) _____ al teléfono rápidamente. (She answers the phone quickly.)
5- ¿Usted (bajar) _____ aquí? (Are you coming down here?)

Exercise 3: Choose the right translation for these sentences.

1- Yo no bebo vino.
   a. I don't drink wine.   b. I never drink wine.   c. I drink wine.

2- Ella ya no trabaja más.
   a. She's always working.   b. She doesn't work.
   c. She doesn't work anymore.

3- Ellos comen muchos chocolates.
   a. They eat a lot of chocolates.   b. He eats a lot of chocolates.
   c. They are eating a lot of chocolates.

4- Andrés trabaja en una fábrica.
   a. Andrés works in a factory.   b. Andrés is working in a factory.
   c. Andrés has been working in a factory.

5- Pedro estudia historia.
   a. Pedro studied history.   b. Pedro studies history.
   c. Pedro is studying history.

Exercise 4: Tick the correct answer.

1- Yo ___ Italiano. (I speak Italian.)
   a. hablo	b. hablan	c. hablas

2- Ellos ___ a Europa. (They travel to Europe.)
   a. viajar	b. viajan	c. viaja

3- Nosotros ___ en Monterrey. (We live in Monterrey.)
   a. vivimos	b. viven	c. vivo

4- Ustedes ___ la televisión. (You watch TV.)
   a. miras	b. miran	c. miro

5- Tú ___ mucho. (You walk a lot.)
   a. caminas	b. caminan	c. camina

Exercise 5: Conjugate the verbs in brackets in the simple present tense.

1- Las ballenas (vivir) _____ en aguas frías. (Whales live in cold waters.)
2- Los argentinos (hablar) _____ español. (Argentinians speak Spanish.)
3- Sara y yo nunca (viajar) _____ en avión. (Sara and I never travel by plane.)
4- Nosotros no (comer) _____ carne. (We don't eat meat.)
5- ¿Dónde (pasar) _____ los veranos usted? (Where do you spend your summers?)

Answers:

Exercise 1

1/ Yo amo mucho esta película. 2/ Ellos trabajan día y noche. 3/ Ella habla muy bien español. 4/ Nosotros comemos fuera esta noche. 5/ ¿Usted paga en efectivo o con tarjeta de crédito?

Exercise 2

1/ Nosotros esperamos el resultado desde la mañana. 2/ ¿Qué ruta tomo para ir al súper? 3/ Ellos venden ropa bonita. 4/ Ella responde al teléfono rápidamente. 5/ ¿Usted baja aquí?

Exercise 3

1/ I don't drink wine. 2/ She doesn't work anymore. 3/ They eat a lot of chocolates. 4/ Andrés works in a factory. 5/ Pedro studies history.

Exercise 4

1/ Yo hablo italiano. 2/ Ellos viajan a Europa. 3/ Nosotros vivimos en Monterrey. 4/ Ustedes miran la televisión. 5/ Tú caminas mucho.

Exercise 5

1/ Las ballenas viven en aguas frías. 2/ Los argentinos hablan español. 3/ Sara y yo nunca viajamos en avión. 4/ Nosotros no comemos carne. 5/ ¿Dónde pasa usted los veranos?

Lesson 9: The past tense – El pasado

Spanish tenses can be complicated and cause countless headaches to any learner. While learning the complicated ins and outs of each of the different tenses is necessary to really take your Spanish to a more fluent level, taking it slow and making sure to master each tense individually is a great way to start!

Let's get started with the past tense so we can describe things that happened in the past, whether in a specific or in an unspecified moment.

Spanish has *three* ways to refer to things that took place in the past, and knowing which one to use can be challenging.

Listen to Track 93

Preterite – This is used when the action in the past happened one time or within a specified period of time.

Example: *Viví en Argentina durante 6 meses.* (I lived in Argentina for six months.)

Imperfect – This is used for actions in the past that took place multiple times or during a period of time that isn't specified.

Example: *Siempre iba a este café.* (He always went to this cafe.)

Present Perfect – This conjugation is a combination of the verb *haber* and the past participle of the verb (ending in *-ado* or *-ido*). This is the one we've previously called the perfect tense. Its use differs throughout the Spanish-speaking world and in Mexico it's not very common. However, generally, you use this tense when the event in the past still has an impact on the present.

Example: *He pagado la cuenta.* (I have paid the bill.)

While the three tenses mentioned above seem relatively cut-and-dry on the surface, they regularly trip up the non-native Spanish speaker. With practice, though, you'll find yourself becoming more familiar with them.

There is, however, one little shortcut you can use to refer to something that happened in the near past. This is using the verb *acabar*. It's like the English equivalent of saying "just."

Using *acabar* to talk about the near past

To use this verb to talk about the near past you will use the following pattern:

Acabar + de + verb in infinitive

This is referring to something that you "just" did, or that was "just" done by someone else. *Acabar* is a regular -*ar* verb.

Listen to Track 94

Yo acabo de

Tú acabas de

Él/ Ella/ Usted acaba de

Nosotros acabamos de

Ustedes acaban de

Ellos/ Ellas/ acaban de

Here are some examples of this verb describing events in the near past:

Listen to Track 95

First person singular: *Acabo de leer ese libro.* (I just read that book.)

Second person singular: *Acabas de regresar de la tienda.* (You just came from the store.)

Third person singular: *Acaba de hacer la cena.* (He/she just made dinner.)

First person plural: *Acabamos de comer.* (We just ate.)

Second person plural: *Acaban de volver de vacaciones.* (You [plural] just returned from vacation.)

Third person plural: *Acaban de comprar los boletos.* (They just bought the tickets.)

Useful verbs in past tense

Listen to Track 96

- *ir* (to go)

Yo fui	Nosotros fuimos
Tú fuiste	Ustedes fueron
Él/ella fue	Ellos/ellas fueron

Listen to Track 97

- **hacer** (to do/to make)

Yo hice	Nosotros hicimos
Tú hiciste	Ustedes hicieron
Él/ella hizo	Ellos/ellas hicieron

Listen to Track 98

- **ser** (to be)

Yo fui	Nosotros fuimos
Tú fuiste	Ustedes fueron
Él/ella fue	Ellos/ellas fueron

Listen to Track 99

- **estar** (to be)

Yo estuve	Nosotros estuvimos
Tú estuviste	Ustedes estuvieron
Él/ella estuvo	Ellos/ellas estuvieron

Listen to Track 100

- **haber** (to have)

Yo hice	Nosotros hicimos
Tú hiciste	Ustedes hicieron
Él/ella hizo	Ellos/ellas hicieron

Listen to Track 101

- **tener** (to have)

Yo tuve	Nosotros tuvimos
Tú tuviste	Ustedes tuvieron
Él/ella tuvo	Ellos/ellas tuvieron

Listen to Track 102

- **poner** (to put)

Yo puse	Nosotros pusimos
Tú pusiste	Ustedes pusieron
Él/ella puso	Ellos/ellas pusieron

Listen to Track 103

- **decir** (to say)

Yo dije	Nosotros dijimos
Tú dijiste	Ustedes dijeron
Él/ella dijo	Ellos/ellas dijeron

Listen to Track 104

- **ver** (to see)

Yo vi	Nosotros vimos
Tú viste	Ustedes vieron
Él/ella vio	Ellos/ellas vieron

Listen to Track 105

- **saber** (to know something/to taste)

Yo supe	Nosotros supimos
Tú supiste	Ustedes supieron
Él/ella supo	Ellos/ellas supieron

Listen to Track 106

- **venir** (to come)

Yo vine	Nosotros vinimos
Tú viniste	Ustedes vinieron
Él/ella vino	Ellos/ellas vinieron

Listen to Track 107

- **conocer** (to know someone)

Yo conocí	Nosotros conocimos
Tú conociste	Ustedes conocieron
Él/ella conoció	Ellos/ellas conocieron

Listen to Track 108

- **dar** (to give)

Yo di	Nosotros dimos
Tú diste	Ustedes dieron
Él/ella dio	Ellos/ellas dieron

Listen to Track 109

- **salir** (to go out)

Yo salí	Nosotros salimos
Tú saliste	Ustedes salieron
Él/ella salió	Ellos/ellas salieron

Listen to Track 110

- **empezar** (to start)

Yo empecé	Nosotros empezamos
Tú empezaste	Ustedes empezaron
Él/ella empezó	Ellos/ellas empezaron

Listen to Track 111

- **pensar** (to think)

Yo pensé	Nosotros pensamos
Tú pensaste	Ustedes pensaron
Él/ella pensó	Ellos/ellas pensaron

Listen to Track 112

- ***preferir*** **(to prefer)**

Yo preferí	Nosotros preferimos
Tú preferiste	Ustedes prefirieron
Él/ella prefirió	Ellos/ellas prefirieron

Listen to Track 113

- ***repetir*** **(to repeat)**

Yo repetí	Nosotros repetimos
Tú repetiste	Ustedes repitieron
Él/ella repitió	Ellos/ellas repitieron

Listen to Track 114

- ***pedir*** **(to ask for)**

Yo pedí	Nosotros pedimos
Tú pediste	Ustedes pidieron
Él/ella pidió	Ellos/ellas pidieron

Workbook Lesson 9: The past tense – El pasado

Exercise 1: Conjugate the verbs into preterite tense.

1- Yo _____ (empezar)
2- Tú _____ (poder)
3- Nosotros _____ (venir)
4- Él _____ (saber)
5- Ustedes _____ (ver)

Exercise 2: Use the correct form of the past tense shortcut with the following sentences.

1- Ayer por la mañana (ir) _____ a una cafetería muy buena.
2- Anoche (salir y tomar) _____ unas copas de vino.
3- Anoche no (dormir) _____ nada.
4- (Terminar) _____ la tarea hace un momento.
5- (Trabajar) _____ en esa compañía por 3 años.

Exercise 3: Tick the correct answer.

1- Yo ___ a España. (I went to Spain.)
   a. iré   b. fue   c. fui

2- Ellos ____ a mi mamá. (They saw my mom.)
   a. vimos   b. veron   c. vieron

3- Nosotros ___ más tarde. (We started later.)
   a. empezamos   b. empiezamos   c. empezaremos

4- ¿Ustedes ___ esa película? (Did you watch that movie?)
   a. viron   b. vieron   c. visto

5- ¿Tú ___ en carro? (Did you come by car?)
   a. viniste   b. vinió   c. vinimos

Exercise 4: Choose the right translation for these sentences.

1- No te vi anoche.
   a. I will see you tonight.   b. I did not see you last night.
   c. You saw me last night.

2- Ella no supo qué decir.
   a. She didn't know what to say.   b. She didn't know who talked.
   c. She didn't talk to me.

3- Ellos pensaron lo mismo.
   a. They thought wrong.   b. He thought wrong.
   c. They thought the same.

4- Cecilia pidió un café.
   a. Cecilia asked for a coffee.   b. Cecilia didn't ask for a coffee.
   c. Cecilia lost her coffee.

5- María me dió el libro.
   a. María sold me her book.   b. María gave me the book.
   c. María did not give me the book.

Answers:

Exercise 1

1/ Yo empecé 2/ Tú pudiste 3/ Nosotros vinimos 4/ Él supo 5/ Ustedes vieron

Exercise 2

1/ Fui 2/ Salí y tomé 3/ Dormí 4/ He terminado/terminé 5/ Trabajé

Exercise 3

1/ Yo fui a España. 2/ Ellos vieron a mi mamá. 3/ Nosotros empezamos más tarde. 4/ ¿Ustedes vieron esa película? 5/ ¿Tú viniste en carro?

Exercise 4

1/ I did not see you last night. 2/ She didn't know what to say.
3/ They thought the same. 4/ Cecilia asked for a coffee.
5/ María gave me the book.

Lesson 10: The future tense – El futuro

Learning to talk about the future in Spanish is pretty easy for the native English speaker. This is because the different options available are similar to their English equivalents.

Listen to Track 115

Using the present – This is used for events that will happen in the near future. To use this conjugation to refer to the future in Spanish, you <u>must</u> specify the time it will happen.

Example: *Nos vamos mañana.* (We leave tomorrow.)

Future conjugation – This is like saying "will" in English and its use is similar to that of the "will" future in English, although in spoken Spanish it isn't as common.

Example: *Más tarde iré a la tienda.* (I will go to the store later.)

The last way that you can use to speak about the future in Spanish is probably the most common, and, conveniently enough, the easiest to learn! This is with the verb *ir*.

Ir a to talk about the future

Using the verb *ir*, meaning "to go," to talk about the future is extremely common, especially in everyday, colloquial speech. It's like the English "going to…"

To use this verb, you will use the following pattern:

Ir + a + verb in infinitive

Ir is irregularly conjugated. It's conjugated as follows:

Listen to Track 116

Yo voy a

Tú vas a

Él/Ella/Usted va a

Nosotros vamos a

Ustedes van a

Ellos/Ellas van a

Some examples of using these constructions are:

Listen to Track 117

First person singular: *Voy a ir a la fiesta.* (I'm going to go to the party.)

Second person singular: *Vas a tener que estudiar mucho.* (You're going to need to study a lot.)

Third person singular: *Va a comprar el pan.* (He/she is going to buy the bread.)

First person plural: *Vamos a viajar a Grecia.* (We're going to travel to Greece.)

Second person plural: *Van a comer en la casa.* (You [plural] are going to eat at home.)

Third person plural: *Van a sacar al perro.* (They are going to walk the dog.)

Useful verbs in future tense

Listen to Track 118

- *ir* (to go)

Yo iré	Nosotros iremos
Tú irás	Ustedes irán
Él/ella irá	Ellos/ellas irán

Listen to Track 119

- *hacer* (to do/to make)

Yo haré	Nosotros haremos
Tú harás	Ustedes harán
Él/ella hará	Ellos/ellas harán

Listen to Track 120

- *ser* (to be)

Yo seré	Nosotros seremos
Tú serás	Ustedes serán
Él/ella será	Ellos/ellas serán

Listen to Track 121

- ***estar*** (to be)

Yo estaré	Nosotros estaremos
Tú estarás	Ustedes estarán
Él/ella estará	Ellos/ellas estarán

Listen to Track 122

- ***haber*** (to have)

Yo habré	Nosotros habremos
Tú habrás	Ustedes habrán
Él/ella habrá	Ellos/ellas habrán

Listen to Track 123

- ***tener*** (to have)

Yo tendré	Nosotros tendremos
Tú tendrás	Ustedes tendrán
Él/ella tendrá	Ellos/ellas tendrán

Listen to Track 124

- ***poner*** (to put)

Yo pondré	Nosotros pondremos
Tú pondrás	Ustedes pondrán
Él/ella pondrá	Ellos/ellas pondrán

Listen to Track 125

- ***decir*** (to say)

Yo diré	Nosotros diremos
Tú dirás	Ustedes dirán
Él/ella dirá	Ellos/ellas dirán

Listen to Track 126

- **ver** (to see)

Yo veré	Nosotros veremos
Tú verás	Ustedes verán
Él/ella verá	Ellos/ellas verán

Listen to Track 127

- **saber** (to know something/to taste)

Yo sabré	Nosotros sabremos
Tú sabrás	Ustedes sabrán
Él/ella sabrá	Ellos/ellas sabrán

Listen to Track 128

- **venir** (to come)

Yo vendré	Nosotros vendremos
Tú vendrás	Ustedes vendrán
Él/ella vendrá	Ellos/ellas vendrán

Listen to Track 129

- **conocer** (to know someone)

Yo conoceré	Nosotros conoceremos
Tú conocerás	Ustedes conocerán
Él/ella conocerá	Ellos/ellas conocerán

Listen to Track 130

- **dar** (to give)

Yo daré	Nosotros daremos
Tú darás	Ustedes darán
Él/ella dará	Ellos/ellas darán

Listen to Track 131

- **salir** (to go out)

Yo saldré	Nosotros saldremos
Tú saldrás	Ustedes saldrán
Él/ella saldrá	Ellos/ellas saldrán

Listen to Track 132

- **empezar** (to start)

Yo empezaré	Nosotros empezaremos
Tú empezarás	Ustedes empezarán
Él/ella empezará	Ellos/ellas empezarán

Listen to Track 133

- **pensar** (to think)

Yo pensaré	Nosotros pensaremos
Tú pensarás	Ustedes pensarán
Él/ella pensará	Ellos/ellas pensarán

Listen to Track 134

- **preferir** (to prefer)

Yo preferiré	Nosotros preferiremos
Tú preferirás	Ustedes preferirán
Él/ella preferirá	Ellos/ellas preferirán

Listen to Track 135

- **repetir** (to repeat)

Yo repetiré	Nosotros repetiremos
Tú repetirás	Ustedes repetirán
Él/ella repetirá	Ellos/ellas repetirán

Listen to Track 136

- ***pedir*** (to ask for)

Yo pediré	Nosotros pediremos
Tú pedirás	Ustedes pedirán
Él/ella pedirá	Ellos/ellas pedirán

Workbook Lesson 10: Future tense – El futuro

Exercise 1: Conjugate the verbs into future tense.

1- Yo _____ (empezar)
2- Tú _____ (poder)
3- Nosotros _____ (venir)
4- Él _____ (saber)
5- Ustedes _____ (ver)

Exercise 2: Use the correct form of the future tense shortcut with the following sentences.

1- (Ir) _____ a Río de Janeiro el próximo año.
2- (Comprar) _____ un nuevo celular.
3- Más tarde, (Llamar) _____ a mi mamá.
4- (Ver) _____ a mis padres el próximo mes.
5- El próximo año, (Tener) _____ un mejor trabajo.

Exercise 3: Tick the correct answer.

1- Yo ___ a ver a mi mamá. (I will go see my mom.)
   a. iré   b. fue   c. fui

2- Ellos ___ muy tarde del concierto. (They will leave the concert late.)
   a. salierán   b. saldrán   c. salió

3- Nosotros ___ un breve discurso. (We will give a brief speech.)
   a. dimos   b. damos   c. daremos

4- Ustedes ___ a toda mi familia (You will meet my entire family.)
   a. conocerán   b. conoció   c. conocieron

5- Tú ___ un muy buen futuro si estudias medicina. (You will have a great future if you study medicine.)
   a. teniste   b. tendrás   c. vinimos

Exercise 4: Identify the tense used in each sentence.

1- Iré a tomar una siesta.
2- Mi papá come plátano todos los días.
3- Los estudiantes rompieron la silla.
4- Vivimos en Colombia por 5 años.
5- El perro ladra.

Exercise 5: Rewrite the sentences by using "acabo de" and "voy a" depending on the case.

1- Me comí una hamburguesa hace un momento.

2- Comeré huevos mañana.

3- Viajo a Orlando el próximo mes.

4- Terminé de limpiar hace un minuto.

5- Llegué hace 30 segundos.

Answers:

Exercise 1

1/ Yo empezaré 2/ Tú podrás 3/ Nosotros vendremos 4/ Él sabrá 5/ Ustedes verán

Exercise 2

1/ Iré 2/ Compraré 3/ llamaré 4/ Veré 5/ tendré

Exercise 3

1/ iré 2/ saldrán 3/ daremos 4/ conocerán 5/ tendrás

Exercise 4

1/ Future tense 2/ Present tense 3/ Past tense 4/ Past tense 5/ Present tense

Exercise 5

1/ Acabo de comer una hamburguesa hace un momento. 2/ Voy a comer huevos mañana. 3/ Voy a viajar a Orlando el próximo mes. 4/ Acabo de terminar de limpiar hace un minuto. 5/ Acabo de llegar hace 30 segundos.

Lesson 11: Asking questions – Hacer preguntas

If any conversation is going to go very far, you have to know how to ask questions. Asking questions isn't only good for that, though. If you travel through a Spanish speaking country, you may want to get information such as "where are the bathrooms?" and "how much does this cost?"

This lesson will give you a quick guide to the different rules, structures, and important vocabulary you should know when asking questions in Spanish.

The Basics

Let's start at the beginning. Like in English, we have two options for asking questions in Spanish. The first is with a "question word." The other is by changing a statement into a question by shifting around the words and/or changing the intonation of your voice.

The way questions are written in Spanish is quite unique. You've already seen the "¿" and now you're going to use it! In Spanish, there will be the inverted question mark at the beginning of the question, and the normal one at the end.

Listen to Track 137

¿Qué quieres hacer? – What do you want to do?

Questions with Question Words

Let's start with how to ask questions in Spanish using question words, or "interrogatives." These are words that make a statement a question. For example, in English we can say "Where is the train station?" In this example, "where" is our question word, letting the listener know we are asking for information.

In Spanish, our question words are:

- *Qué* - What
- *Dónde* - Where
- *Cuánto/a* - How much
- *Cuántos/as* - How many
- *Por qué* - Why
- *Cuál* - Which
- *Quién* - Who
- *Cómo* - What
- *Cuándo* - When

You'll notice that ALL of these words have accents! If they are used in a statement, they do not have the accent, but the pronunciation stays the same.

Listen to Track 138

Example:

¿Dónde está Pedro? ¡No sé donde está! (Where is Pedro? I don't know where he is!)

Generally speaking, the verb goes right after the question word.

¿Por qué tengo que ir? (Why do I have to go?)

¿Dónde está la biblioteca? (Where is the library?)

¿Cómo está? (How is he/she/it? OR How are you (singular/formal)?)

You'll notice that with some questions, it's pretty clear what we're talking about. With others, however (the last in the list above, for example), unless we can infer it from the conversation, we need to specify a little. If this is the case, the subject will come after the verb.

¿Cómo está ella? (How is she?)

¿Cómo está usted? (How are you [singular/ formal]?)

Word Order and Intonation

Sometimes you may have a question that doesn't use a question word. This is very common in both Spanish and English. So, let's look at how those would be formed.

In Spanish, like in English, we can also create questions by moving around the words. However, there is a little more freedom in Spanish as to where those words should go.

For example, the question "Is she going to the store?" could be said:

Listen to Track 139

¿Va a la tienda? – no subject because due to the conversation we're all aware we're talking about the subject "she."

The following are ways of putting in the subject for specification or emphasis. This is because the verb conjugation can go with any number of subjects (he, she, it, you).

¿Va ella a la tienda?

¿Ella va a la tienda?*

You'll notice that in English, we use an auxiliary or "helping" verb ("is") whereas in Spanish we do not. To form the question in Spanish, the helping verb isn't required.

Or, the question "Do you want to go to the movies?" could be said:

¿Quieres ir al cine? – There's no subject because the conjugation tells us who we are talking about.

The following are examples <u>with</u> the subject. Note: when we have a verb conjugated to a subject that can only be one thing (i.e. "tú," "yo," "nosotros," "ustedes") we add in the subject, more often than not, because we want to emphasize it. The following are like saying "*You* want to go to the movies? (as in, you *never* want to go to the movies, and I'm surprised!).

¿Quieres ir tú al cine?

¿Tú quieres ir al cine?*

* These questions have word orders that are identical to their statement forms. In these cases it is very important to use the correct intonation, or the listener will be confused.

You'll notice here that the auxiliary verb "do" in English acts as another type of "question word." Other than turning the statement "you want to go to the movies" into the question "do you want to go to the movies?" It has no other purpose. In Spanish, we don't have this type of construction. We simply change the order of the words, and make sure our intonation goes up, up, up at the end of our question.

One last thing…

Listen to Track 140

You can also take a statement and turn it into a question by adding a sort of "question tag" to the end. For Example: "You're coming tonight, right?"

Vienes esta noche, ¿verdad?

Notice how the question marks only go around the part of the statement that is the question.

Tienes que estudiar, ¿no? (You have to study, no?)

Voy a la fiesta, ¿y tú? (I'm going to the party, are you?)

Asking questions in Spanish isn't unlike asking questions in English. It's just important to remember your intonation.

Word order is a little more relaxed, and (other than the "question words" we looked at before) you don't have to worry about throwing in any "helping" words along the way. The best way to become more familiar and comfortable with asking questions is simple ... by doing it! So, get out there and practice, practice, practice!

Workbook Lesson 11: Asking questions – Hacer preguntas

Exercise 1: Change these statements into questions.

1- Usted ama Argentina. (You like Argentina.)
   _____

2- Es su perro. (It's your dog.)
   _____

3- Usted habla español. (You speak Spanish.)
   _____

4- Él es un buen amigo. (He's a good friend.)
   _____

5- Ella ha llegado. (She arrived.)
   _____

Exercise 2: Complete these questions with the right question words.

1- ¿_____ cuesta este teléfono? (How much does this phone cost?)
2- ¿_____ hermanos y hermanas tienes? (How many brothers and sisters do you have?)
3- ¿_____ están mis zapatos nuevos? (Where are my new shoes?)
4- ¿_____ le hago para ir a la estación de tren? (How do I go to the train station?)
5- ¿_____ te gustan los perros? (Why do you like dogs?)

Exercise 3: Choose the correct translation.

1- Do you like cats?
   a. ¿Qué gato te gusta?
   b. ¿Por qué te gustan los gatos?
   c. ¿Te gustan los gatos?

2- Where is he?
   a. ¿Dónde está él?
   b. ¿Cuándo va a llegar él?
   c. ¿Quién es él?

3- Did you eat lunch today?
   a. ¿Has comido hoy?
   b. ¿Quisieras comer hoy?
   c. ¿Cuándo es que has comido hoy?

4- Who sings this song?
   a. ¿Quién canta esta canción?
   b. ¿Quién cantó esa canción?
   c. ¿Dónde se canta esta canción?

5- Which one of you is María?
   a. ¿Quién de ustedes es María?
   b. ¿Cuál de ustedes es María?
   c. ¿Quién es María?

Exercise 4: Tick the right answer.

1- ¿____ ha llamado por teléfono? (Who called on the phone?)
   a. Cuál   b. Quién   c. Cómo

2- ¿____ vende esa señora? (What is that lady selling?)
   a. Qué   b. Quién   c. Cuáles

3- ¿____ son los ganadores? (Who are the winners?)
   a. Quiénes   b. Quién   c. Cuándo

4- ¿____ tienes en la mano? (What do you have in your hand?)
   a. Quién   b. Qué   c. Cuál

5- ¿____ viven Andrés y María? (Where do Andrés and María live?)
   a. Cuándo   b. Dónde   c. Quién

Exercise 5: Translate these sentences from English to Spanish.

1- Which are the Hispanic countries?
   _____

2- Who is Camila's father?
   _____

3- How old is Andrés?
   _____

4- Why is he always late?
   _____

5- Where do you come from?
   _____

Answers:

Exercise 1

1/ ¿Ama usted Argentina? 2/ ¿Es su perro? 3/ ¿Habla usted español? 4/ ¿Es él un buen amigo? 5/ ¿Ha llegado ella?

Exercise 2

1/ ¿Cuánto cuesta este teléfono? 2/ ¿Cuántos hermanos y hermanas tienes? 3/ ¿Dónde están mis zapatos nuevos? 4/ ¿Cómo le hago para ir a la estación de tren? 5/ ¿Por qué te gustan los perros?

Exercise 3

1/ ¿Te gustan los gatos? 2/ ¿Dónde está él? 3/ ¿Has comido hoy? 4/ ¿Quién canta esta canción? 5/ ¿Quién de ustedes es María?

Exercise 4

1/ Quién 2/ Qué 3/ Quiénes 4/ Qué 5/ Dónde

Exercise 5

1/ ¿Cuáles son los países hispanos? 2/ ¿Quién es el padre de Camila? 3/ ¿Cuántos años tiene Andrés? 4/ ¿Por qué él siempre llega tarde? 5/ ¿De dónde vienen ustedes?

Lesson 12: The verbs "to be" – Ser y estar

One of the most important verbs in English is the verb "to be." Well, "to be" in Spanish is just as important, but there are two Spanish verbs that both mean "to be": *ser* and *estar*.

Although they both mean "to be," they aren't the same and can't be used interchangeably. That's where this lesson comes in!

A simple rule for the difference between when to use *ser* or *estar* is that *ser* is for permanent things, and *estar* is for temporary things. However, the rules go so much deeper than that, and we want you to be able to use the right verb at the right time!

Listen to Track 141

Ser

Conjugation

First of all, let's learn how to conjugate *ser* in the present tense. It's very irregular.

yo	soy
tú	eres
él/ella/usted	es
nosotros	somos
ustedes	son
ellos/ ellas	son

When to use *ser*

A common device for learning the uses of *ser* is to remember the acronym "**DOCTOR**." Each letter stands for a situation where you'd use *ser*.

D = Descriptions

Listen to Track 142

This refers to the permanent or essential qualities of a person or object. Let's look at some examples.

Soy Juan.	I'm Juan.
Eres un hombre guapo.	You are a handsome man.
Ana es una chica.	Ana is a girl.
Somos altos.	We are tall.
¿Son ingleses?	Are you guys English?
Los coches son negros.	The cars are black.

O = Occupations

Listen to Track 143

When you're saying what someone does, use *ser*. It could be a job or just something that they do as a hobby.

Soy médico.*	I'm a doctor.
Eres pianista.	You're a pianist.
Jaime es mesero en un gran restaurante.	Jaime is a waiter in a big restaurant.
Tenemos muchos exámenes porque somos estudiantes.	We have lots of exams because we're students.
Señores, ¿son bomberos?	Gentlemen, are you firefighters?
Pedro y Paula son enfermeros.	Pedro and Paula are nurses.

*Note that in Spanish, you don't have to use "a" or "an" before an occupation. You say "*soy médico*" rather than "*soy un médico.*"

C = Characteristics

We said earlier that *ser* is used for descriptions, and this includes the characteristics of someone's personality.

Listen to Track 144

Yo soy flojo.	I am lazy.
Eres una persona feliz.	You are a happy person.
Andrés es aventurero.	Andrés is adventurous.
Somos amables.	We are nice.
Son muy graciosos.	You (plural) are very funny.
Las chicas de mi clase son inteligentes.	The girls in my class are intelligent.

T = *Time*

When you're talking about time, use *ser*. This doesn't just mean times of the day—it also includes days, months, etc.

Listen to Track 145

Ya son las tres.	It's already three o'clock.
Hoy es viernes.	Today is Friday.
¡Es mi cumpleaños!	It's my birthday!
Es marzo.	It's March.

O = *Origins*

Listen to Track 146

We use *ser* to talk about the origin of something or someone. This includes what something is made of.

Soy de Colombia.	I'm from Colombia.
Eres de Argentina, ¿verdad?	You're from Argentina, right?
La puerta es de madera.	The door is made of wood.
La guitarra es de México.	The guitar is from México.

R = *Relations*

Listen to Track 147

When you're describing how people are related to each other, use *ser*.

Soy la tía de Pedro.	I'm Pedro's aunt.
Eres mi novio.	You are my boyfriend.
Lupita es mi abuela.	Lupita is my grandmother.
Pepe es el hermano de Pedro.	Pepe is Pedro's brother.

Listen to Track 148

Estar

Conjugation

Here's how to conjugate *estar* in the present tense:

yo	estoy
tú	estás
él/ella/usted	está
nosotros	estamos
ustedes	están
ellos/ellas	están

When to use *estar*

A useful way to remember when to use *estar* is the acronym "**PLACE**."

P = *Position*

We use *estar* to say where something is, or how it's positioned.

Listen to Track 149

Estoy a tu lado.	I'm by your side.
¿Estás en frente del hotel?	Are you in front of the hotel?
La biblioteca está al lado del mercado.	The library is next to the market.
Estamos acostados en el parque.	We are lying in the park.
Están sentados.	You (plural) are sitting/seated.
Mis padres están cerca.	My parents are nearby.

L = *Location*

Listen to Track 150

Estar is used to talk about the place that someone or something is in. In other words, a person or thing's location, whether it's temporary or permanent!

Estoy en el baño.	I'm in the bathroom.
¿Estás?	Are you there?
La estación está a tu derecha.	The station is on your right.
Estamos en Nueva York.	We're in New York.
Están en mi casa.	You (plural) are in my house.
Los perros están en el jardín.	The dogs are in the yard.

There is an exception to this one. When you're saying where an event is being held, you use *ser*. So, you would say *"la fiesta es en mi casa"* rather than *"la fiesta está en mi casa."*

A = *Action*

Estar is used in the gerund, and can be used in past, present, future, etc. This is when you want to say what someone is do**ing**, e.g. he is swimm**ing**, she was sing**ing**, he'll be laugh**ing**, etc.

Listen to Track 151

Estoy pensando en él.	I'm thinking about him.
Estás bailando.	You are dancing.
Camila está cambiando el mundo.	Camila is changing the world.
María y yo estamos buscando departamento.	María and I are looking for an apartment.
Chicos, ¿están caminando o corriendo?	Boys, are you walking or running?
Señoras, ¿están esperando?	Ladies, are you waiting?

C = *Condition*

When talking about a physical or emotional condition that is changeable (as opposed to personality traits, which are pretty much set), use *estar*.

For example:

Listen to Track 152

Estoy mareado.	I'm feeling dizzy.
Mamá, ¿estás lista?	Mom, are you ready?
Carla está enamorada de Lucía.	Carla is in love with Lucía.
Estamos muy cansados.	We are very tired.
Puedo ver que están enfermos hoy.	I can see that you're (plural) unwell today.
Ayer mis abuelos estaban confundidos.	Yesterday my grandparents were confused.

E = *Emotion*

This one is self-explanatory: use *estar* for emotional states.

Listen to Track 153

Estoy aburrida en esta clase.	I am bored in this class.
¿Estás contento?	Are you happy?
Camila está feliz porque está con su hermana.	Camila is happy because she's with her sister.
Ambos estamos muy emocionados (o: Los dos estamos muy emocionados).	We are both very excited.
Se ve que están tristes por sus calificaciones.	It's clear that you (plural) are feeling sad about the grades.
Tus amigos están preocupados por ti.	Your friends are worried about you.

Words that change meaning

Interestingly, some adjectives can be used with *ser* or *estar*, but then they have different meanings. Sometimes the difference is subtle and linked to the permanence of the adjective, and sometimes there's quite a big difference in meaning.

It's tricky but helpful to learn them. Some of the common ones are in the table below.

Listen to Track 154

Ser aburrido (to be boring)	*Estar aburrido* (to be bored)
Ser un enfermo (to be chronically ill)	*Estar enfermo* (to be unwell)
Ser feliz (to be happy - personality trait)	*Estar feliz* (to be happy - a temporary state)
Ser frío (to be cold - personality trait)	*Estar frío* (to be cold - current temperature)
Ser guapo (to be good-looking)	*Estar guapo* (to be looking good now)
Ser listo (to be smart/clever)	*Estar listo* (to be ready)
Ser malo (to be bad)	*Estar malo* (to be ill)
Ser orgulloso (to be proud - as a person; could have negative connotation)	*Estar orgulloso* (to be proud of someone or something)
Ser rico (to be rich)	*Estar rico* (to be tasty)
Ser seguro (to be safe)	*Estar seguro* (to be sure)
Ser verde (to be green)	*Estar verde* (to be unripe)
Ser viejo (to be old)	*Estar viejo* (to be looking old)
Ser vivo (to be quick/sharp)	*Estar vivo* (to be alive)

Be careful with these ... the last thing you want is to try and say you're rich but accidentally claim to be tasty!

Well done!

If you've followed this lesson, then you've done well, as the differences between *ser* and *estar* can be subtle. They need practice, so do a little bit of Spanish every day and you'll see the improvement!

Workbook Lesson 12: The verbs "to be" – Ser y estar

Exercise 1: Choose the correct form of the verb "ser" in the present tense.

1- Él _____ un chico bueno. (He is a nice kid.)
2- Nosotros _____ italianos. (We are Italian.)
3- Ustedes _____ muy guapos (You are very good looking.)
4- Ellas _____ hermanas. (They are sisters.)
5- Él _____ buena persona (He is a good person.)

Exercise 2: Conjugate the verb "estar" in the present tense.

1- Este café _____ muy caliente. (This coffee is so hot.)
2- Este árbol _____ muerto. (This tree is dead.)
3- Hoy no _____ feliz. (I am not happy today.)
4- Este libro _____ roto. (This book is broken.)
5- Mi ropa _____ sucia. (My clothes are dirty.)

Exercise 3: Complete this dialogue with the right form of the verb "estar" or "ser."

Pedro: Buenos días, ¿ _____ aquí Maria? (Hello, is Maria there?)

La mamá de María: No, ella no _____ . _____ en el doctor con su papá. Ellos _____ enfermos. ¿Quieres dejarle un mensaje? ¿Tú _____ ? (No, she's not here. She went to the doctor with her dad. They are both sick. Do you want to leave a message for her? You are...?)

Pedro: Pedro. _____ Pedro. Sí, muchas gracias. (Pedro. I am Pedro. Yes, thank you very much.)

Exercise 4: Translate these sentences from English to Spanish.

1- I am Mexican.   - _____
2- He is tall.   - _____
3- They are doctors. (m.) - _____
4- We are smart.   - _____
5- You are nice. (pl.) - _____

Exercise 5: Tick the correct answer.

1- Andrés ____ muy delgado. (Omar is very thin.)
   a. estamos   b. está   c. estoy

2- Yo ___ en Perú. (I'm in Peru.)
   a. está   b. estoy   c. están

3- Carla y Luis ____ de luna de miel. (Carla and Luis are on their honeymoon.)
   a. estamos   b. están   c. estoy

4- Estos cristales ____ muy sucios. (These crystals are very dirty.)
   a. están   b. estamos   c. estás

5- Esta comida ____ deliciosa. (This food is delicious.)
   a. estoy   b. está   c. están

Answers:

Exercise 1

1/ Él es un chico bueno. 2/ Nosotros somos italianos. 3/ Ustedes son muy guapos. 4/ Ellas son hermanas. 5/ Él es buena persona.

Exercise 2

1/ Este café está muy caliente. 2/ Este árbol está muerto. 3/ Hoy no estoy feliz. 4/ Este libro está roto. 5/ Mi ropa está sucia.

Exercise 3

Pablo: Buenos días, ¿está aquí María? (Hello, is Maria there?)

La mamá de María: No, ella no está. Está en el doctor con su papá. Ellos están enfermos. ¿Quieres dejarle un mensaje? ¿Tú eres...? (No, she's not here. She went to the doctor with her dad. They are both sick. Do you want to leave a message for her? You are...?

Pedro: Pedro. Soy Pedro. Sí, muchas gracias. (Pedro. I am Pedro. Yes, thank you very much.)

Exercise 4

1/ Yo soy mexicano. 2/ Él es alto. 3/ Ellos son médicos/doctores. 4/ Nosotros somos inteligentes. 5/ Ustedes son amables.

Exercise 5

1/ está 2/ estoy 3/ están 4/ están 5/ está

Lesson 13: Singular and plural nouns – Sustantivos singulares y plurales

¡Buenos días! Today we're looking at how to make singular nouns plural! The only background knowledge you need is that when we say a noun is "singular," it means there's only one of them. When we refer to it as "plural," there's more than one.

We've made a list of rules to help you form all sorts of plurals, but generally it's pretty simple.

Rule #1: Change the article

The first rule is that when you make a singular noun plural, you must remember to change the article that goes with it, for example *la chica* becomes *las chicas*.

Here's how to change the common articles, with examples:

Listen to Track 155

Singular article	Plural article
El	*Los*
El chico (the boy)	*Los chicos* (the boys)
La	*Las*
La chica (the girl)	*Las chicas* (the girls)
Un	*Unos*
Un chico (a boy)	*Unos chicos* (some boys)

Rule #2: Add an -s when it ends in a vowel

When a Spanish noun ends in an unstressed vowel, it's a simple case of adding an -s to the end of it.

Listen to Track 156

Un perro (one dog)	*Dos perros* (two dogs)
Una manzana (one apple)	*Dos manzanas* (two apples)

Rule #3: Add an -s when it ends in -é or -ó

We've seen what to do with unstressed vowels, and if the vowel at the end of the noun has an accent (-é or -ó), the noun also becomes plural by adding -s, just like in Rule #2.

Listen to Track 157

Un café (a coffee)	*Dos café***s** (two coffees)
La mesa de café (the coffee table)	*Las mesas de café* (the coffee tables)

Rule #4: Add -es if it ends in -á, -í, or -ú (exceptions apply)

If a noun ends in -á or -í or -ú, we usually add -es.

Listen to Track 158

El rubí (the ruby)	*Los rubí***es** (the rubies)
El bambú (the bamboo)	*Los bambú***es** (the bamboos)

There are exceptions to this rule. Some of these nouns (such as *mamá* and *menú*, and a lot of other common nouns) form their plurals irregularly – we just add an -s.

Listen to Track 159

La mamá y el papá (the mommy and the daddy)	*Las mamá***s** *y los papá***s** (the mommies and the daddies)
El menú (the menu)	*Los menú***s** (the menus)

Rule #5: Add an -es when it ends in a consonant other than s

The general rule for words ending in consonants is that we add -es.

Listen to Track 160

El color (the color)	*Los color***es** (the colors)
La ciudad (the city)	*Las ciudad***es** (the cities)
Un rey (one king)	*Cinco rey***es** (five kings)

Rule #6: If the noun ends in -s, leave it as it is

As long as there's no stress on the final syllable, the noun remains unchanged in the plural.

Listen to Track 161

El Jueves (Thursday)	*Los Jueves* (Thursdays)
El virus (the virus)	*Los virus* (the viruses)
El cactus (cactus)	*Los cactus* (cacti)

This rule often applies to Spanish compound nouns. We're talking about words where a verb and a noun are joined together to make a bigger word, e.g. *paraguas* = *parar* (to stop) + *agua* (water).

Listen to Track 162

Mi paraguas (my umbrella)	*Mis paraguas* (my umbrellas)
Su cumpleaños (his birthday)	*Sus cumpleaños* (his birthdays)

But if the final syllable is stressed ...

Rule #7: Add an *-es* when the noun ends in a stressed vowel + *-s*

If the noun ends in *-s* and the emphasis is on the last syllable when spoken (which will also be the case for words that only have one syllable!), then add *-es*.

Listen to Track 163

El mes (month)	*Los mes**es*** (months)
El autobús* (bus)	*Los autobus**es**** (buses)

*See rule #8 to find out why we removed the accent.

Rule #8: If the noun ends in a consonant and the last syllable has an accent, you can usually remove it

In Spanish, we have rules surrounding stress and emphasis within words. If the noun ends in a consonant, we're most likely going to be adding *-es*, which adds an extra syllable onto the end of the word. This means that we don't need the accent anymore.

Listen to Track 164

Un autobús (a bus)	*Unos autobus**es*** (some buses)
El francés (Frenchman)	*Los frances**es*** (Frenchmen)
Un pantalón (a pair of pants)	*Ocho pantalon**es*** (eight pants)

Rule #9: If the noun ends in *-en*, do the opposite of #8!

Sometimes making a noun plural means we actually have to add an accent, to maintain the stress when we add the new *-es* syllable. This usually applies to words ending in *-en*.

Listen to Track 165

| *El crimen* (the crime) | *Los crímenes* (the crimes) |
| *Una imagen* (an image) | *Unas imágenes* (some images) |

Rule #10: If it's a foreign word, just add *-s*

One of the cool things about languages is that they're always borrowing and adapting words from each other! When a non-Spanish word (or an adapted version of it) is used in Spanish, we usually just add an *-s* to it!

Listen to Track 166

| *El chalet* (chalet) | *Los chalets* (chalets) |
| *Un hacker* (one hacker) | *Dos hackers* (two hackers) |

Rule #11: Families

When we use a surname to talk about members of a family, we don't add *-s* or *-es*, Although royalty is an exception.

Listen to Track 167

| *Soy Ana Smithson.* (I'm Ana Smithson.) | *Somos los Smithson.* (We're the Smithsons.) |
| *Estoy enamorado de una Jones.* (I'm in love with a Jones.) | *Estoy enamorado de una de las Jones.* (I'm in love with one of the Joneses.) |

Rule #12: Some nouns are only ever plural

You don't need to worry about changing these, e.g *las tijeras* (scissors).

Rule #13: Some nouns are only ever singular

You don't need to worry about making these plural, e.g. *el tenis* (tennis). You can have more than one *game of* tennis, but you can't have more than one tennis. These nouns are called mass nouns. They're uncountable.

Rule #14: Spelling changes!

This one is just a quick note on spelling. If the noun in the singular form ends in *-z*, we'll need to change it to a *-c* before we add *-es*.

Listen to Track 168

| *Un pez* (a fish) | *Unos pe***ces** (some fish) |
| *La voz* (the voice) | *Las vo***ces** (the voices) |

Rule #15: To pluralize a noun that is written in both its masculine and feminine way in the same sentence, it is necessary to use the masculine one.

When, for example, you invite one female friend and one male friend to a party, in English it stays the same: "I invited two **friends**." In Spanish, you use the plural ***amigos*** even though you invited ***un amigo*** (male) and ***una amiga*** (female). To summarize, you must pluralize them as if you were only using the masculine (and don't forget the article).

Listen to Track 169

Un ciudadano y una ciudadana (citizen)	*Unos ciudadan***os** (some citizens)
Un amigo y una amiga (friend)	*Unos amig***os** (some friends)
Un niño y una niña (kid)	*Unos niñ***os** (some kids)
El cliente y la clienta (customer)	*Los client***es** (the customers)

Quiz

Try to figure out the plural form of each of the following nouns! The parts in brackets give you the meaning of the singular noun in English, and then the plural that you want to get to. Don't forget to change the article!

1. *El tentempié* (the snack -> the snacks) -_____

2. *El corazón* (the heart -> the hearts) -_____

3. *El lápiz* (the pencil -> the pencils) -_____

4. *El germen* (germ -> germs) -_____

5. *Un guardaespaldas* (one bodyguard -> two bodyguards) -_____

So there are your rules! Now you know how to turn Spanish singular nouns into plurals. ¡Hasta la próxima!

Workbook Lesson 13: Singular and plural nouns – Sustantivos singulares y plurales

Exercise 1: Write the plural of the following nouns.

1- Actriz   - _____
2- Pantalones - _____
3- Camión   - _____
4- Pez   - _____
5- Jueves   - _____

Exercise 2: Choose the correct plural of the following words.

1- calcetín: a. calcetíns   b. calcetines
2- pez: a. peces   b. pezes
3- plátano: a. plátanes   b. plátanos
4- jueves: a. jueves   b. jueveses
5- lámpara: a. lámparas   b. lampares

Exercise 3: Write the plural of the following sentences and phrases:

1- La flor del jardín de María. (Maria's flower garden.)
   _____

2- El frijol mexicano es delicioso. (The Mexican bean is delicious.)
   _____

3- Nuestro mejor cocinero es de Tailandia. (Our best chef is from Thailand.)
   _____

4- Una raíz muy grande. (A huge root.)
   _____

5- El pastel de fresa. (Strawberry cake.)
   _____

Exercise 4: Change these plural nouns into singular ones.

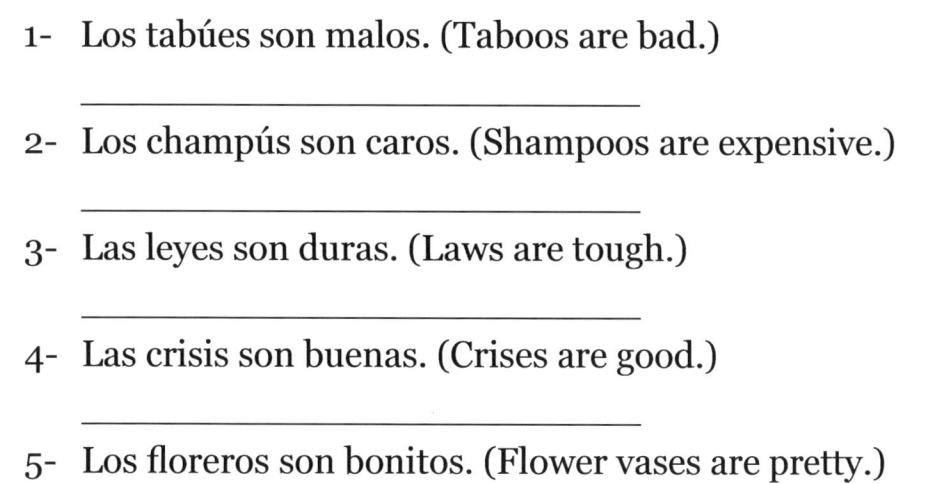

1- Los tabúes son malos. (Taboos are bad.)
_____

2- Los champús son caros. (Shampoos are expensive.)
_____

3- Las leyes son duras. (Laws are tough.)
_____

4- Las crisis son buenas. (Crises are good.)
_____

5- Los floreros son bonitos. (Flower vases are pretty.)
_____

Answers:

Quiz

1/ los tentempiés 2/ los corazones 3/ los lápices 4/ los gérmenes 5/ dos guardaespaldas

Exercise 1

1/ Actrices 2/ Pantalones 3/ Camiones 4/ Peces 5/ Jueves

Exercise 2

1/ calcetines 2/ peces 3/ plátanos 4/ jueves 5/ lámparas

Exercise 3

1/ Las flores del jardín de María. 2/ Los frijoles mexicanos son deliciosos. 3/ Nuestros mejores cocineros son de Tailandia. 4/ Unas raíces muy grandes. 5/ Los pasteles de fresa.

Exercise 4

1/ El tabú no es malo. 2/ El champú no es caro. 3/ La ley no es dura. 4/ La crisis no es buena. 5/ El florero es bonito.

Lesson 14: Adjectives – Adjetivos

Adjectives make a thing more interesting or exciting. They can make a boring sentence dynamic, a nice sentiment sweeter, and a harsh word, well ... even harsher.

If you want to be able to describe something, you need to be able to use this handy, and necessary, part of speech!

In Spanish, adjectives are a little more complicated than they are in English. But don't fret! Below is a quick guide to how you can spice up your conversations.

The Basics

So what are adjectives? Adjectives are the words we add to a sentence to describe our nouns. They *describe* a person, place, thing, or idea.

For example:

   The house – The red house

   The boy – The handsome boy

   The building – The tall building

So, let's look at how these parts of speech work in Spanish.

One thing about Spanish that is very different from English is that words have a gender. They can be "feminine" or "masculine."

If you remember lesson 4, you'll have realized that a lot of words end in -o or -a. Well, the "-o" words are masculine, and the "-a" words are feminine.* Like the nouns they describe, the adjectives will need to be either masculine or feminine too.

For example:

   "The red house" – here, the word "house" in Spanish is feminine (*la casa*) so you will need the *feminine* form of the adjective "red" (*roja*).

*Remember: Not ALL nouns end in either -o or -a. But ALL nouns do have a gender! This is something you have to memorize. **Example:** *coche* (car) – masculine; *leche* (milk) – feminine.

And how many "reds" will you need?

Just like agreeing in gender, your adjectives need to agree in number. If you have more than one house, you will have more than one "red."

For example:

"The red house" – here, we have only one, singular red house, so our adjective would be *roja* (singular). But if we were to say "the red houses," our adjective would become the plural version *rojas*. No matter if we have 2 or 23 red houses – if there is more than one, they will be *rojas*.

I know this seems a little weird, but it's really not all that difficult. Just remember that your adjectives have to AGREE & AGREE!! (Two agreements for two criteria – <u>gender</u>, and <u>number</u>.)

Almost time to put it all together

One more thing ... In Spanish, the adjectives usually follow the noun.

Let's go back to our example:

Listen to Track 170

"The red house" – In Spanish this little phrase would be *"La casa roja."* So, literally you're saying, "The house red."

Examples:

The handsome boy – *El chico* (the boy) *guapo* (handsome/ attractive)

The tall building – *El edificio* (the building) *alto* (tall)

The handsome boys – *Los chicos guapos*

The tall buildings – *Los edificios altos*

The Technicalities

Some adjectives will change ALL the possible forms we looked at briefly above (masculine, feminine, singular, plural) while some won't.

You will find, generally speaking, three different types of adjectives:

- Adjectives that end in "-*o*"

- Adjectives that end in "-*e*"

- Adjectives that end in a consonant

To make this a little easier, let's look at these in a chart.

Listen to Track 171

Adjective	Meaning	Masculine	Feminine	Singular	Plural
Bonit**o**	Pretty	Bonito	Bonita	Bonito(a)	Bonitos(as)
Tímid**o**	Shy	Tímido	Tímida	Tímido(a)	Tímidos(as)
Grand**e**	Big	--------------	--------------	Grande	Grandes
Inteligent**e**	Intelligent	--------------	--------------	Inteligente	Inteligentes
Le**al**	Loyal	--------------	--------------	Leal	Leales
Jov**en**	Young	--------------	--------------	Joven	Jóvenes

As you can see in the chart above, there are a few small differences between the three different types of adjectives you'll find.

- **Adjectives that end in "-o"**

Can be <u>masculine</u> or <u>feminine</u>

Can be <u>singular</u> or <u>plural</u>

Listen to Track 172

The shy boy	El chico tímido	Singular/Masculine
The shy girl	La chica tímida	Singular/Feminine
The shy children	Los chicos tímidos	Plural/Masculine*

- **Adjectives that end in "e"**

These will only change between the <u>singular</u> and <u>plural</u> forms.

To make the plural form, simply add an "s."

Listen to Track 173

The intelligent boy	El chico inteligente	Singular
The intelligent girl	La chica inteligente	Singular (doesn't change)
The intelligent children	Los chicos inteligentes	Plural (no gender)

- **Adjectives that end in a consonant**

These will only change between the singular and plural forms.

To make the plural form, add "es."

Listen to Track 174

The loyal boy	*El chico leal*	Singular
The loyal girl	*La chica leal*	Singular (doesn't change)
The loyal children	*Los chicos leales*	Plural (no gender)

*Note: When describing a group of something, the adjective will become masculine even if only one of the things in the group is masculine. It's the same as in the plurals rule #15, but with adjectives.

Of course, the exceptions...

Like with almost everything when learning a language, this comes with its own little list of exceptions to the rules.

- **Adjectives ending in -or, -án, -ín, -ón**

This group, although they end in consonant, will in fact still have a feminine form.

Listen to Track 175

Example	Meaning	Masculine	Feminine	Singular	Plural
Hablador	Talkative	*Hablador*	*Habladora*	*Hablador(a)*	*Habladores(as)*

- **Adjectives that go before the noun**

There are some adjectives in Spanish that **do** go before the noun they are describing.

The first group of adjectives that you will find coming before the noun are those relating to a quantity. They describe the amount of something.

For example:

Listen to Track 176

Hay poca gente en la casa. (There are a few people in the house.)

- **Adjectives that change meaning when they change location**

There are a handful of adjectives that can go before *or* after the noun, but they will change their meaning depending on where you put them.

The most common are:

Listen to Track 177

Adjective	Meaning before	Meaning after
Antiguo	former, ex-	old, ancient
Pobre	poor (as in *unfortunate*)	poor (as in *no money*)
Gran/Grande	great	big, large
Viejo	old (as in long-*standing*)	old (as in age)
Único	only	unique

This has just been a quick overview of the basics behind using adjectives in Spanish. At first glance, this very useful part of speech may seem strange and even intimidating to the native English speaker. But the truth is, it's really not all that complicated! It just takes lots of practice and adjusting your mindset a little bit.

Remember – your adjectives need to AGREE & AGREE!

Workbook Lesson 14: Adjectives – Adjetivos

Exercise 1: Complete the sentences with the correct form of the adjectives in brackets.

1- Sara tiene los ojos (verde)_____, es (rubio)_____ y tiene el pelo (corto)_____ y (rizado)_____ (Lola has green eyes, is blonde, and has short, curly hair.)
2- Él es muy (simpático) _____, (alegre)_____ y muy (charlatán)_____ (He is very likeable, cheerful, and very talkative.)
3- Las hijas de Andrés son muy (joven)_____ (Andrés's daughters are very young.)
4- Me gustan las rosas (blanco)_____ (I like white roses.)
5- Esta gata está (enfermo)_____ (This cat is sick.)

Exercise 2: Complete the sentences with a noun and an adjective, as in the example.

Example: Este es el chico inteligente. (This is the intelligent boy.)

1- Pedro tiene los _____. (Pedro has blue eyes.)
2- La rosa es una _____. (The rose is a red flower.)
3- Esta computadora es muy _____. (This computer is very old.)
4- Necesito comprar _____. (I need to buy new clothes.)
5- Voy a comprar _____. (I am going to buy Spanish food.)

Exercise 3: Choose the correct adjective for the following sentences.

1- Sara y Camila son muy:
   a. trabajador   b. trabajadoras
2- Me he comprado unos zapatos:
   a. negres   b. negros
3- Pedro y Andrés son:
   a. altos y morenos   b. altes y morenos
4- Él es un hombre:
   a. leale   b. leal
5- Ella es muy:
   a. tímida   b. tímidas

Exercise 4: Translate the following phrases from English to Spanish.

1- The shy children   - _____
2- The kind lady   - _____
3- The intelligent children - _____
4- The old cheerful man - _____
5- The strong man   - _____

Exercise 5: Complete the following dialogue by changing the adjectives.

Camila: Hola Liliana. Mira, esta es mi amiga Sofía, es (Chile) _____.

Liliana: Hola Sofía, mucho gusto, yo soy (Panamá) _____.

Sofía: ¡Mucho gusto! Uff, me gusta mucho vivir en Panamá, hace calor y el clima es muy agradable. La ciudad es muy (bonito) _____, el aire está muy (limpio) _____ y la plaza _____ (antiguo) es muy (bello) _____.

Answers:

Exercise 1

1/ Sara tiene los ojos verdes, es rubia, y tiene el pelo corto y rizado.
2/ Él es muy simpático, alegre y muy charlatán. 3/ Las hijas de Andrés son muy jóvenes. 4/ Me gustan las rosas blancas. 5/ Esta gata está enferma.

Exercise 2

1/ Pablo tiene los ojos azules. 2/ La rosa es una flor roja. 3/ Esta computadora es muy vieja. 4/ Necesito comprar ropa nueva. 5/ Voy a comprar comida china.

Exercise 3

1/ trabajadoras 2/ negros 3/ altos y morenos 4/ leal 5/ tímida

Exercise 4

1/ Los niños tímidos 2/ La señora amable 3/ Los niños inteligentes
4/ El viejo alegre

5/ El hombre fuerte

Exercise 5

Camila: Hola Liliana. Mira, ésta es mi amiga Sofía, es chilena. (Hi Liliana. Look, this is my friend Sofia, she is Chilean.)
Liliana: Hola Sofía, mucho gusto, yo soy panameña. (Hi Sofia, glad to meet you. I am Panamanian.)
Sofía: ¡Mucho gusto! Uff, me gusta mucho vivir en Panamá, hace calor y el clima es muy agradable. La ciudad es muy bonita, el aire está muy limpio y la plaza antigua es muy bella. (Nice to meet you! I really like living in Panama. It's hot and the weather is very nice. And the city is very pretty. The air is very clean and the Old Square is very beautiful.)

Lesson 15: How to tell time – Cómo dar la hora

¡Hola!

Telling the time is an important skill, so today we're learning to tell the time in Spanish. The most important thing you need to know before learning how to tell time is, of course, numbers! We already covered the numbers in Lesson 4, so give it a quick review before getting started with this lesson if you'd like a refresher.

Asking for the Time

Next, we want to know enough vocabulary to ask for the time!

Listen to Track 178

The time/the hour	*La hora*	lah 'oh-rah
Minute	*El minuto*	ehl mee-'noo-toh
Have you got the time?	*¿Tiene(s) la hora?*	tee-'eh-neh(s) lah 'oh-rah
What time is it?	*¿Qué hora es?**	keh 'oh-rah ehs
What time do you make it?	*¿Qué hora tiene(s)?*	keh 'oh-rah tee-'eh-neh(s)
To tell the time	*Decir la hora*	deh-'seer lah 'oh-rah
To ask for the time	*Preguntar la hora*	preh-goon-'tahr lah 'oh-rah

In Mexico and other parts of Latin America you might also hear "¿qué horas son?*", which is also correct. *So feel free to use it, as well as all the other formats.*

To respond to this question, we use the verb *ser* ("to be"). Instead of "*x* o'clock," Spanish speakers count hours.

Example: *Son las 8.* => it is 8 (hours). => it is 8 o'clock.

Usually, you'll need to use "*son las...*" to mean "it is" but occasionally you use "*es la*" (*ehs lah*). This is because "*son las*" is used for plural times, i.e. anything more than 1 o'clock. "*Es la*" is singular, so it's used for 1 o'clock (and x minutes past 1).

O'clock

So, let's have a look at the following times:

Listen to Track 179

It's 1 o'clock.	*Es la una.*
It's 3 o'clock.	*Son las tres.*
It's 6 o'clock.	*Son las seis.*
It's 11 o'clock.	*Son las once.*

Bonus:

Usually, when we say "it's 12 o'clock," we know whether it's the middle of the day or the middle of the night, but sometimes we prefer to make it extra clear:

Listen to Track 180

It's midday.	*Es mediodía.*	ehs meh-dee-oh-'dee-ah
It's midnight.	*Es medianoche.*	ehs meh-dee-ah-'noh-cheh

Half past

When it's half past the hour, we use "*y media,*" (*ee 'meh-dee-ah*) which means "and half." See if these examples make sense:

Listen to Track 181

It's 1:30.	*Es la una y media.*
It's 5:30.	*Son las cinco y media.*
It's 7:30.	*Son las siete y media.*
It's 12:30.	*Son las doce y media.*

Quarter past

To say that it's quarter past the hour, we add "*y cuarto*" (*ee 'kwahr-toh*), which means "and a quarter."

Listen to Track 182

It's 1:15.	*Es la una y cuarto.*
It's 4:15.	*Son las cuatro y cuarto.*
It's 8:15.	*Son las ocho y cuarto.*
It's 10:15.	*Son las diez y cuarto.*

Quarter to

Like in English, we can still use the word for "quarter." If we say it as the literal translation *cuarto a la una* (*'kwahr-toh ah lah 'oo-nah*), it's perfect. But in Mexico there are also two other versions that mean the same thing:

Listen to Track 183

"***Falta*** *un cuarto para las x.*" There's a missing quarter to x (where is it ?!)

"***Es*** *cuarto para las x.*" Use the verb "to be" (*ser*) to complement.

It's 12:45 (quarter to one).	*Falta un cuarto para la una.*
It's 1:45 (quarter to two).	*Es cuarto para las dos.*
It's 8:45 (quarter to nine).	*Es cuarto para las nueve.*
It's 9:45 (quarter to ten).	*Falta un cuarto para las diez.*

Minutes past

For highly specific numbers (i.e. not quarters or halves), we have a pretty simple rule! We just say the "o'clock" bit and then add the number of minutes past the hour!

Listen to Track 184

It's 1:23.	*Es la una veintitrés.*
It's 1:47.	*Es la una cuarenta siete.*
It's 4:05.	*Son las cuatro cinco.*
It's 4:59.	*Son las cuatro cincuenta y nueve.*
It's 6:11.	*Son las seis once.*

Minutes to

Listen to Track 185

And for minutes **to** the hour, we use "*para la/las...*" (*pahrah lah/lahs*) or "*a la/las...*" (*ah lah/lahs*). You just have to say how many minutes are left.

It's 12:55 (five minutes to one).	*(Son) cinco **para la** una.*
It's 8:52 (8 minutes to 9).	*(Son) ocho **a las** nueve.*
It's 2:45 (15 minutes to 3).	*(Son) quince **a las** tres.*
It's 11:40 (20 minutes to 12).	*(Son) veinte **para las** doce.*

In Mexico, this format is used when there aren't many minutes left to the next hour (max. 25 minutes).

A few extras:

Listen to Track 186

The morning	*La mañana*	la mah-'nyah-nah
It's 8 in the morning/8am.	*Son las ocho de la mañana.*	
The afternoon	*La tarde*	lah 'tahr-deh
It's 2 in the afternoon/2pm.	*Son las dos de la tarde.*	
The evening/night	*La noche*	lah 'noh-cheh
It's 11 at night/11pm.	*Son las once de la noche.*	
The early hours of the morning	*La madrugada*	lah mah-droo-'gah-dah
Go to sleep! It's 2am!	*¡Duérmete! ¡Son las dos de la madrugada!*	
… and a bit.	*… y pico**	ee 'peeh-koh
It's a few minutes past 7.	*Son las siete y pico.*	
Around	*Alrededor de / más o menos*	ahl-reh-deh-'dohr deh mahs oh 'meh-nohs
It's around 5.	*Son alrededor de las cinco.* *Son las cinco más o menos.*	
On the dot.	*En punto.*	ehn 'poon-toh
It's 6 on the dot.	*Son las seis en punto.*	
At …	*A la/las …*	ah lah/lahs
We cook at 2.	*Cocinamos a las dos.*	
The party starts at 1.	*La fiesta empieza a la una.*	

* "Y pico / Y algo" is understood as a "a few minutes past," but it could also refer to anything up to around 50 minutes past the hour.

12-hour vs. 24-hour clock

Depending on where you're from, you may be more used to the 12-hour clock than the 24-hour clock (military time). In Spanish-speaking destinations, you could encounter both. Like in English, spoken Spanish tends to use the 12-hour clock, even if the time is sometimes written in the 24-hour format. For example, if you were reading out theater times, the page in front of you might say "15:00," but you'd say, "It starts at three."

Mini-test

It's **time** for a mini-test! See if you can figure out what the following phrases mean.

Listen to Track 187

1. *Es la una.*

2. *Es mediodía.*

3. *Son las tres y media.*

4. *Son las cuatro y cuarto.*

5. *Falta un cuarto para las siete.*

6. *Son las ocho diez.*

7. *Son cinco a las nueve.*

8. *Son las once en punto.*

9. *Son las once de la mañana.*

Keep practicing

Whether you've struggled with this or found it pretty easy, practicing Spanish daily will help you get to grips with telling the time. Numbers are used often in everyday life, so the more you speak, the more opportunities you'll get to practice them! If you know any native Spanish-speakers, try and practice what you've learned with them.

Spanish Calendar Vocabulary: Days and Months in Spanish

Now let's learn Spanish words relating to the calendar!

In this lesson, we'll discover Spanish words for the different days of the week and the months, as well as how to talk about dates in Spanish.

The basics

Before we go to the different names of days and months, let's learn some basic words first.

Listen to Track 188

El calendario	Calendar
El día	Day
La semana	Week
El mes	Month
La fecha	Date

The days of the week

Let's think about the days of the week (*los días de la semana*).

Listen to Track 189

lunes	Monday
martes	Tuesday
miércoles	Wednesday
jueves	Thursday
viernes	Friday
sábado	Saturday
domingo	Sunday

Unlike in English, the names of the days of the week are not capitalized in Spanish. Let's see some examples below.

Listen to Track 190

Necesito ir al médico el jueves. (I need to go to the doctor on Thursday.)

Mi cumpleaños es el martes. (My birthday is on Tuesday.)

El nuevo capítulo sale cada miércoles. (The new chapter comes out every Wednesday.)

Voy a la iglesia el domingo. (I go to church on Sunday.)

Months in Spanish

Now let's move on to the different months of the year.

Listen to Track 191

enero	January
febrero	February
marzo	March
abril	April
mayo	May
junio	June
julio	July
agosto	August
septiembre	September
octubre	October
noviembre	November
diciembre	December

Just like the days of the week, the names of the months are not capitalized in Spanish!

Let's take a look at some example sentences below.

Listen to Track 192

El cumpleaños de Luis es en febrero. (Luis's birthday is in February).

Las vacaciones terminan en septiembre. (Vacation ends in September).

Mi boda será en enero. (My wedding will be in January).

Talking about dates in Spanish

Dates will always come up in conversations, so make sure you know how to say the date in Spanish!

Here are a few useful notes:

The format for saying dates in Spanish is: *el* + day + *de* + month (+ *del* [from 2000] + year).

For example:

Listen to Track 193

Hoy es el nueve de enero. (Today is January 9.)

El dos de septiembre del 2015. (September 2, 2015.)

*You only use "*el*" when you are talking about a past event or something that hasn't happened yet, so if someone asks you: When was the party? You answer "**el** *10 de diciembre.*"

Cardinal numbers (*dos, tres*) are used when talking about dates in Spanish, except for the first day of the month, where an ordinal number is needed.

Listen to Track 194

Example:

Hoy es primero de enero. (Today is January 1st.)

Here are some more examples:

*Hoy es 5 de diciembre **del** 2018.* (Today is December 5, 2018.)

*Ella nació **el** 12 de febrero **de** 1990.* (She was born on February 12, 1990.)

*Nuestra primera cita fue **el** 10 de julio **del** 2018.* (Our first date was on July 10, 2018.)

Workbook Lesson 15: How to tell time – Cómo decir la hora

Exercise 1: Write the right time in Spanish from the following phrases.

1- It's 1:20. - _____
2- It's 6:30. - _____
3- It's 7 o'clock. - _____
4- It's 11:15. - _____
5- It's 5:45 (quarter to six). - _____

Exercise 2: Fill the gaps with the correct days of the week.

1- Antes del martes está el _____
2- Antes del sábado está el _____
3- Antes del jueves está el _____
4- Antes del miércoles está el _____
5- _____, sábado, domingo

Exercise 3: Reorder the letters in each word to discover the hidden month.

1- LUJIO: - _____
2- TOGOSA: - _____
3- ROEEN: - _____
4- SBREEPTMIE: - _____
5- YMAO: - _____

Exercise 4: Complete the next exercise with the correct month.

1- La navidad siempre es en _____.
2- El verano empieza en _____.
3- _____ es el primer mes del año.
4- Me gusta _____ por las flores hermosas.
5- San Valentín es en _____.

Exercise 5: Rearrange the following words into a sentence.

1- cumpleaños / el / de / pedro / es / en marzo
2- la final / de / en julio/ la liga / es
3- yo termino / en noviembre / mis /estudios
4- ellos / en octubre / se casaron
5- el / febrero / es / carnaval de Río / en

Answers:

Mini-test

1/ It's 1:00. 2/ It's midday. 3/ It's 3:30. 4/ It's 4:15. 5/ It's 6:45. 6/ It's 8:10. 7/ It's 8:55. 8/ It's exactly 11./11 on the dot. 9/ It's 11am.

Exercise 1

1/ Es la una veinte 2/ Son las seis y media 3/ Son las siete en punto 4/ Son las once y cuarto 5/ Son quince a las seis

Exercise 2

1/ Lunes 2/ Viernes 3/ Miércoles 4/ Martes 5/ Viernes, sábado, domingo

Exercise 3

1/ Julio 2/ Agosto 3/ Enero 4/ Septiembre 5/ Mayo

Exercise 4

1/ La navidad siempre es en diciembre. 2/ El verano empieza en junio. 3/ Enero es el primer mes del año. 4/ Me gusta abril por las flores hermosas. 5/ San Valentín es en febrero.

Exercise 5

1/ El cumpleaños de Pedro es en marzo. 2/ La final de la liga es en julio. 3/ Yo termino mis estudios en noviembre. 4/ Ellos se casaron en octubre. 5/ El carnaval de Río es en febrero.

Lesson 16: Negatives – La negación

It's time to get negative! Using negatives in Spanish is important and can make your language seem a lot more sophisticated, so let's look at how to do it.

Double negatives in Spanish are okay!

When making negative statements in Spanish, you can either use *no* (which means "no" or "not"), or you can use a negative word, or both together!

Don't let the apparent double negatives confuse you. We're taught in English not to use double negatives, because a negative and a negative make a positive, so using it can get quite confusing (and grammatically incorrect), for example:

I have**n't** got **nothing**. (I have actually got something.)

But in Spanish, a negative and a negative remain negative!

Listen to Track 195

No tengo **nada**. (I haven't got anything./ I've got nothing.)

Word order

The basic rule is that we put the *no* before the main verb in the phrase. If there are pronouns, then stick it in front of those. The other negative word (if applicable) goes right after the verb.

Listen to Track 196

| **No** voy a la biblioteca. | I don't go to the library. |
| **No** voy **nunca** a la biblioteca. | I never go to the library. |

When using a compound tense (the perfect, the pluperfect, etc.), you still put the *no* before the verbs. You then put the other negative word **after both** verbs.

Listen to Track 197

| **No** he dicho **nada**. | I haven't said anything. |
| **No** había venido **nadie**. | No one had arrived. |

Earlier we said that negative words usually need to be used with *no* as well. However, sometimes it will be more natural to use the negative word alone, without *no*. In this case, you'd put the negative word before the verb(s).

Listen to Track 198

No cantó nadie. → *Nadie cantó.*	Nobody sang.
No bailas nunca. → *Nunca bailas.*	You never dance.

Another simple way to use negatives is as one-word answers.

Listen to Track 199

—*¿Quieres tomar algo conmigo?* —*No.*	—Do you want to get a drink with me? —No.
—*¿Qué haces?* —*Nada.*	—What are you doing? —Nothing.
—*¿Has estado alguna vez en Brasil?* —*¡Nunca!*	—Have you ever been to Brazil? —Never!

Listen to Track 200

- **No**

This can simply mean "no," or it can mean "not" when used to negate statements. Put it at the beginning of a phrase, before the verb, and before pronouns if there are any.

—*¿Vienes a la fiesta?* —*No.*	—Are you coming to the party? —No.
Hay fruta en casa.	There's fruit at home.
No hay fruta en casa.	There isn't fruit at home.
Lo sé.	I know.
No lo sé.	I don't know.
Me lo dio.	He gave it to me.
No me lo dio.	He didn't give it to me.

Sometimes, *no* is used as a question tag. We can make a statement then stick a *no* on the end, to see if the person you're talking to agrees or not.

Listen to Track 201

Ana es muy inteligente, ¿no?	Ana is very intelligent, isn't she?
Has hecho la tarea, ¿no?	You've done the homework, haven't you?
La clase es mañana, ¿no?	The class is tomorrow, right?

Listen to Track 202

- **Ni... ni...**

This means "neither... nor...." It's the negative opposite of *o... o...* ("either... or...").

| *Ni canto ni bailo.* | I neither sing nor dance. |
| *No canto ni bailo.* | I don't sing or dance. |

Listen to Track 203

- **Nada**

Nada means "nothing." It's the negative opposite of *algo* ("something').

No dije nada.	I didn't say anything.
No hay nada en el refri.	There is nothing in the refrigerator.
Nada nos puede separar.	Nothing can separate us.

Listen to Track 204

- **Nadie**

This one means "no-one" or "nobody." Its opposite would be *alguien* ("someone"/ "somebody").

¿No viste a nadie?	You didn't see anyone?
No hay nadie en el equipo que me pueda ayudar.	There is no one on the team who can help me.
Aquí nadie se rinde.	Nobody quits here.

Listen to Track 205

- **Ninguno/a/os/as**

Ninguno means "not any." It's called an "indefinite adjective," and it describes a noun.

When it's used before a masculine singular noun, *ninguno* becomes *ningún*.

Listen to Track 206

No hay ninguna mujer en el edificio.	There aren't any /there are no women in the building.
No hay ningún hombre aquí.	There aren't any/there are no men here.
Ningún hombre en esta oficina sabe qué hacer en esta situación.	No man (none of the men) in this office knows what to do in this situation.

Listen to Track 207

- **Ninguno/a/os/as**

Similar to the above, this one means "not one of / none." This is an "indefinite pronoun," and it's slightly different as it's used as a replacement for the noun.

There's no shortening to *ningún* in this case.

—¿Cuál chico prefieres?	—Which guy do you prefer?
—Pues ninguno.	—Well, neither/none.
—¿Tienes ideas?	—Do you have any ideas?
—No, no tengo ninguna.	—No, I don't have any/I have none.

Listen to Track 208

- **Nunca/Jamás**

Usually, *nunca* and *jamás* mean "never" (although they can also be used in the sense of "ever") and their opposite is *siempre* (always).

No voy nunca a su casa.	I never go to her house.
Nunca vienes a mi casa.	You never come to my house.

Listen to Track 209

- **Tampoco**

Last but not least, this one means "(n)either." It's the opposite of *también* ("also').

Ella no va tampoco/Ella tampoco va.	She's not going either.
—No quiero salir con David.	—I don't want to go out with David.
—Yo tampoco.	—Me neither.
Tampoco quiere salir con nosotras.	Nor does he want to go out with us /He doesn't want to go out with us either.

Workbook Lesson 16: Negatives – La negación

Exercise 1: Change these affirmative sentences into negative ones.

1- Yo amo las manzanas. (I love apples.)
   _____

2- Él hace deporte. (He plays sports.)
   _____

3- Ellos están casados. (They are married.)
   _____

4- El vestido es rojo. (The dress is red.)
   _____

5- Ella trabaja aquí. (She works here.)
   _____

Exercise 2: Change these negative sentences into affirmative ones.

1- Esa falda no es verde. (This skirt is not green.)
   _____

2- Esta película no es mala. (This movie is not bad.)
   _____

3- Ellos no son malos. (They are not mean.)
   _____

4- Este trabajo no es difícil. (This work is not hard.)
   _____

5- Yo no estoy cansado. (I am not tired.)
   _____

Exercise 3: Choose the right translation for these sentences.

1- Él nunca ha manejado.
   a. He always drove.
   b. He never drove.
   c. He doesn't drive.

2- Ella no trabaja más.
   a. She's always working.
   b. She doesn't work.
   c. She doesn't work anymore.

3- Yo no conozco a nadie aquí.

   a. I know everybody here.
   b. I don't know anybody here
   c. I don't know anymore.

4- Yo no tengo suficiente dinero para comprar una casa.

   a. I don't have enough money to buy a house.
   b. I have enough money to buy a house.
   c. I don't have enough money to buy a house anymore.

5- Yo no tengo nada que darte.

   a. I have nothing to give you.
   b. I have nothing to give you anymore.
   c. I have something to give you.

Exercise 4: Complete these sentences with "No," "Nunca," "Nada," or "Nadie."

1- Me encantaba esta película, pero ahora ya _____ me gusta más. (I liked this movie before. Now, I don't like it anymore.)

2- Me gustaría viajar. Yo _____ lo he hecho. (I would like to travel. I've never done it.)

3- No he hecho _____ en todo el día. (I've done nothing all day long.)

4- ¿Dónde está la gente? No veo a _____ aquí. (Where are the people? I don't see anyone here.)

5- Ayer lavé los platos. Hoy _____ los he lavado. (Yesterday, I washed the dishes. Today, I didn't do it.)

Exercise 5: Tick the correct answer.

1- Ellos ____ saben cocinar. (They don't know how to cook.)
   a. nadie   b. no   c. nunca

2- Martin ____ está en casa (Martin is not at home.)
   a. nunca   b. no   c. nadie

3- ____ aquí entiende este tema. (Nobody here understands this topic.)
   a. No   b. Nadie   c. Nunca

4- ____ puedes fumar aquí. (You cannot smoke here.)
   a. No   b. Nadie   c. Nunca

5- ____ debes hablar por teléfono aquí. (You mustn't talk on the phone here.)
   a. Nunca   b. Nadie   c. No

Answers:

Exercise 1

1/ Yo no amo las manzanas. 2/ Él no hace deporte. 3/ Ellos no están casados. 4/ El vestido no es rojo. 5/ Ella no trabaja aquí.

Exercise 2

1/ Esa falda es verde. 2/ Esta película es mala. 3/ Ellos son malos. 4/ Este trabajo es difícil. 5/ Yo estoy cansado.

Exercise 3

1/ He never drove. 2/ She doesn't work anymore. 3/ I don't know anybody here. 4/ I don't have enough money to buy a house. 5/ I have nothing to give you.

Exercise 4

1/ no 2/ nunca 3/ nada 4/ nadie 5/ no

Exercise 5

1/ no 2/ no 3/ Nadie 4/ No 5/ No

Lesson 17: Prepositions – Preposiciones

Prepositions are small words that pack a big punch. They define, identify, and explain, and are an essential part of everyday speech.

They help you identify the girl <u>with</u> the long hair, and you need them to explain that dinner is <u>on</u> the table. It's almost impossible to say a single sentence <u>without</u> one of these useful little words!

Learning to use prepositions in Spanish isn't overly difficult, but does take some practice. Read on for a quick introduction to these very useful little words.

What are prepositions and why are they so important?

A preposition is a (usually) little word that can have a big impact on what you're saying. It is what forms the connections and relations between different elements in a sentence.

For example (prepositions in bold):

The girl **from** Cuba

The boy **across** the street

The store **in** the mall

They can be very important because there's a big difference between saying, "The dog is on the table" and "the dog is under the table" or "the dog is in the table."

Prepositional Phrases

A preposition is always followed by an object (a noun or pronoun). In the examples given previously, the <u>prepositional phrases</u> would be:

The girl <u>from Cuba</u>

The boy <u>across the street</u>

The store <u>in the mall</u>

Prepositions in Spanish

Prepositions in Spanish function much as they do in English. They always take an object, and they serve as either an adverb or adjective.

While on the surface they appear pretty easy, sometimes they can cause a few problems. Mainly, this comes when deciding which preposition to use when.

For example, one of the prepositions that gets misused frequently in Spanish by English speakers is *en*.

Listen to Track 210

Spanish	English	Examples
En	in, on, at	*Estoy en la tienda.* *Está en la mesa.* *Estoy en la casa de un amigo.*

Two of its uses are pretty easy (in, on) since it sounds like its English equivalents.

Estoy en la tienda. (I'm in the store.)

Está en la mesa. (It's on the table.)

This little word causes problems, however, with its third meaning, "at." Often, as English speakers, we want to use the Spanish preposition *a* in place of *en* because we associate the *a* with our own "at." This is wrong, though.

For example:

Estoy en la casa de un amigo. (I'm at a friend's house.)

Let's look at some of the most common prepositions in Spanish and their different meanings and uses.

Most Common Prepositions in Spanish

In addition to *en*, which we've already seen, you will also commonly hear/see the following prepositions in Spanish:

Listen to Track 211

Spanish	English	Examples
A	to, at (for time)	*Voy a la tienda.* (I'm going to the store.) *Estaré ahí a las tres.* (I'll be there at 3:00.)
Antes de	before	*Debes estirar antes de hacer ejercicio.* (You should stretch before doing exercise.)
Cerca de	near	*Estamos cerca de tu casa.* (We are near your house.)
Con	with	*Ella está con sus padres.* (She is with her parents.)

De	of, from (indicating possession)	*¿Qué piensas de la nueva película?* (What do you think of the new movie?) *Soy de Estados Unidos.* (I am from the USA.) *Estamos en (la) casa de María.* (We are at Maria's house.)
Adentro de (Dentro de)	inside	*Mi coche está adentro del garaje.* (My car is inside the garage.)
Desde	since, from	*No he estado ahí desde hace un mes.* (I haven't been there since last month.) *Tiró la pelota desde aquí.* (He threw the ball from here.)
Después de	after	*Después de clase, voy a estudiar.* (After class, I'm going to study.)
Detrás de (Atrás de)	behind	*El pan está detrás de los huevos.* (The bread is behind the eggs.) *La mochila está atrás del sillón.* (The backpack is behind the couch.)
Durante	during	*Durante el vuelo, dormí.* (During the flight, I slept.)
Encima de	on top of	*La sal está encima de la mesa.* (The salt is on the table.)
Enfrente de	opposite, across from	*Nos veremos enfrente de la biblioteca.* (We'll meet across from the library). *Note: This is another one that usually trips up English speakers since it sounds like our version of "in front of." If you want to say "We'll meet <u>in front</u> of the library" it would be *Nos veremos <u>en (at)</u> la biblioteca.*
Entre	between, among	*Entre nosotros (nos), no me gusta el profesor de inglés.* (Between us, I don't like the English teacher.) *Hay un traidor entre nosotros.* (There's a traitor among us.)
Fuera de (Afuera de)	outside	*Los baños están (a)fuera de la estación.* (The restrooms are outside the station.)

Hasta	until	*No llegaré hasta las seis.* (I won't arrive until 6:00.)
Para	for, in order to	*Compré el regalo para ti.* (I bought the gift for you.)
		Para aprender español, tienes que estudiar mucho. (In order to learn Spanish, you have to study a lot.)
Por	for, by, through	*Les damos las gracias por su paciencia.* (We are thankful for your patience.)
		El Quijote fue escrito por Cervantes. (*Don Quijote* was written by Cervantes.)
		Tenemos que atravesar por el parque para llegar a la escuela. (We have to pass through the park in order to get to the school.)
Sin	without	*No puedo vivir sin ti.* (I can't live without you.)
Sobre	over, about	*El avión vuela sobre el océano.* (The plane flies over the ocean.)
		El libro es sobre la Guerra Civil. (The book is about the Civil War.)

Some tricky verb/ preposition combinations

Now that we have a working list of the most common prepositions in Spanish, let's look at some of the verb/preposition combinations that can be more difficult for English speakers.

A lot of verbs in Spanish take a specific preposition. For example:

Listen to Track 212

Empezar a- to start

Acabar de- to finish

Dejar de- to quit

The best way to learn these is simply by familiarizing yourself with them as you come across them. Below, however, is a list of those that seem to be common pitfalls for English speakers because we would probably use a different preposition with the verb.

Contractions in Spanish

There are only two contractions in Spanish, and they both happen to relate to prepositions. So, let's just go ahead and take a quick look at those, shall we?

Listen to Track 213

A+el = Al

Whenever you find these two words (*a* and *el*) next to each other, you merge them into one!

Quiero ir a el cine = Quiero ir al cine. (I want to go to the movies.)

De+el = Del

You can do the same thing if you come across these two words (*de* and *el*) together.

Vengo de el dentista = Vengo del dentista. (I'm coming from the dentist.)

On the surface, Spanish prepositions appear to be just like the ones in English. However, there are a few little nuances that every English-speaking Spanish student should be familiar with. These little, but extremely useful, words can be confusing sometimes. But, don't worry! The more you practice them, the easier they become.

Workbook Lesson 17: Prepositions – Preposiciones

Exercise 1: Complete the sentences with the appropriate prepositions.

1- Despiértame _____ las ocho. (Wake me up at eight.)
2- Los domingos solo trabajo _____ la mañana. (I only work in the morning on Sundays.)
3- Mi cumpleaños es el 30 _____ noviembre. (My birthday is November 30.)
4- Ana no puede estudiar _____ la noche, se duerme. (Anna cannot study at night – she falls asleep.)
5- Podemos vernos _____ las siete. (We can meet at seven.)

Exercise 2: Complete the sentences with the corresponding prepositions using *a, hasta, desde, de,* or *dentro de* to create the expressions in brackets.

1- Trabajé en una empresa mexicana _____ el año pasado. (I worked for a Mexican company until last year.)
2- Patricio vive en la Ciudad de México _____ 2003. (Patricio has lived in Mexico City since 2003.)
3- Los bancos abren _____ ocho _____ cuatro. (Banks open from eight to four.)
4- Quiero ir a México _____ dos meses. (I want to go to Mexico in two months.)
5- Katia lleva enferma _____ el martes. (Katia has been sick since Tuesday.)

Exercise 3: Complete the sentences using *antes de, durante,* or *después de.*

1- Camilo estuvo hablando _____ toda la clase. (Camilo was speaking throughout the class.)
2- Estábamos agotados _____ nadar en en el mar. (We were exhausted after swimming at the beach.)
3- Cristina estaba muy nerviosa _____ la entrevista. (Cristina was very nervous during the interview.)
4- Me quedé muy relajado _____ de tomar un baño. (I was very relaxed after the shower.)
5- Hay que tener los teléfonos apagados _____ los conciertos. (You have to keep your phones off during concerts.)

Exercise 4: Complete the sentences with the correct word from the following: *con, de, a, sobre, en* **or** *entre.*

1- Hay dos fotos _____ el piano. (There are two pictures above the piano.)
2- Esperanza está _____ su padre y su madre. (Esperanza is with his father and mother.)
3- Cartagena está _____ Colombia. (Cartagena is in Colombia.)
4- Gira por la primera _____ la izquierda. (Turn at / take the first left.)
5- Hay unas nubes _____ el pueblo. (There are clouds over the village.)

Exercise 5: Complete the following sentences using *con, contra,* **or** *sin.*

1- Quiero un café _____ leche. (I want a latte.)
2- No puedes irte _____ permiso. (You cannot leave without permission.)
3- El salmón nada _____ corriente. (The salmon swims against the current.)
4- Es difícil manejar _____ lluvia. (It is difficult to drive in the rain.)
5- No puedes tener una fiesta _____ pastel. (You can't have a party without cake.)

Exercise 6: Complete the sentences using *por, para, sin, con, contra,* **or** *según.*

1- He recibido los documentos _____ correo. (I received the documents by mail.)
2- Es difícil hacer esta traducción _____ diccionario. (It is difficult to do this translation without a dictionary.)
3- Necesitamos cortinas _____ la habitación. (We need curtains for the room.)
4- Hace frío, no salgas _____ abrigo. (It's cold, don't go out without a coat.)
5- Están buscando una vacuna _____ el COVID-19. (They're looking for a COVID-19 vaccine.)

Answers:

Exercise 1

1/ a 2/ en 3/ de 4/ por 5/ a

Exercise 2

1/ Trabajé en una empresa mexicana hasta el año pasado. 2/ Patricio vive en la Ciudad de México desde 2003. 3/ Los bancos abren de ocho a cuatro.
4/ Quiero ir a México dentro de dos meses. 5/ Katia lleva enferma desde el martes.

Exercise 3

1/ Camilo estuvo hablando durante toda la clase. 2/ Estábamos agotados después de nadar en el mar. 3/ Cristina estaba muy nerviosa durante la entrevista.
4/ Me quedé muy relajado después de tomar un baño. 5/ Hay que tener los teléfonos apagados durante los conciertos.

Exercise 4

1/ Hay dos fotos sobre el piano. 2/ Esperanza está con su padre y su madre.
3/ Cartagena está en Colombia. 4/ Gira por la primera a la izquierda.
5/ Hay unas nubes sobre el pueblo.

Exercise 5

1/ Quiero un café con leche. 2/ No puedes irte sin permiso. 3/ El salmón nada contra corriente. 4/ Es difícil manejar con lluvia. 5/ No puedes tener una fiesta sin pastel.

Exercise 6

1/ He recibido los documentos por correo. 2/ Es difícil hacer esta traducción sin diccionario. 3/ Necesitamos cortinas para la habitación. 4/ Hace frío, no salgas sin abrigo. 5/ Están buscando una vacuna contra el COVID-19.

Lesson 18: When to use "por" vs. "para"

Por and *para* both translate into English as "for," but they can't be used interchangeably! In this lesson we'll show you when to opt for *por* and when to pick *para*.

The way some people like to look at it is that *por* is used for looking back to the cause or origin of something, and *para* is used for forward-looking things (like purpose or destination). But this is a massive generalization, and we want you to understand the difference in more detail.

When to use *para*

Let's look at *para* first, as it has fewer complicated uses than *por*!

[Sometimes, in more colloquial speech, you're likely to hear *para* shortened to *pa*. Listen for it in Spanish movies and songs!]

- **Final goal/destination/purpose/object**

One of the main uses of *para* is to talk about the final goal or purpose of something.

Listen to Track 214

—¿Para qué es esto?	What is this for?
—Es para limpiar los platos.	It's for washing dishes.
Una mesa para tres, por favor.	A table for 3 (people), please.
Come verduras para mantenerse sano.	He eats vegetables to stay healthy.
Compré algo para ti.	I bought something for you.

- **Advantage or disadvantage**

When something is good/bad for someone/something.

Listen to Track 215

Beber demasiado alcohol es malo para la salud.	Drinking too much alcohol is bad for the health.
Eres muy importante para mí.	You are very important to me.

- **Deadline**

We use *para* to express that something needs to be done by a certain time.

Listen to Track 216

| La tarea es para el martes. | The homework is for Tuesday. |
| Necesito un vestido para mañana. | I need a dress for/by tomorrow. |

- **Direction after motion verbs**

We can use *para* to say where we're headed.

Listen to Track 217

| Este camión va para las montañas. | This bus is going to the mountains. |
| Voy para la casa. | I'm going home. |

- **Reaction/response**

Use *para* to say that a certain reaction or feeling is being had by a specific person.

Listen to Track 218

| Para mí, huele a fresa. | To me, it smells of strawberry. |
| Para Pedro, Diana es perfecta. | In Pedro's eyes, Diana is perfect. |

- **Considering**

When we want to say "for" in the sense of "considering" or "given," we use *para*.

Listen to Track 219

| Sofía lee bien para su edad. | Sofía reads well for her age. |

- **Para + infinitive = in order to**

We can use *para* with an infinitive, to mean "in order to."

Listen to Track 220

| Me lo compré para usarlo en la fiesta. | I bought it to wear to the party. |
| Marcos estudia para pasar los exámenes. | Marcos studies (in order) to pass his exams. |

When to use *por*

As we've mentioned, *por* is often used when talking about the root or cause of something. It's used in various ways, as we'll explain below. Some of the categories are very similar, and may overlap, but looking at a variety of situations will help you get the picture!

BONUS: After looking at these examples, the phrase *¿por qué?* should now make sense, as it literally means "for what?"

- **Cause**

The first use we'll look at is cause. When something is the cause of something else, we can use *por* to mean "because of."

Listen to Track 221

Vengo a Barcelona por su arquitectura.	I come to Barcelona for/because of its architecture.
Las flores murieron por falta de sol.	The flowers died for/due to lack of sunlight.

This can include emotional states. Let's say you're feeling sad because you've just done an exam and you feel it hasn't gone very well.

Listen to Track 222

—¿Por qué estás triste?	Why are you sad?
—Por el examen.	Because of the exam.

- **How something works**

We use *por* to explain how something works or happens, in the sense that it happens through/by means of something, always writing *medio de* (means of) after *por*. Otherwise, it may not make sense.

Listen to Track 223

El avión vuela por medio de la física.	The airplane works thanks to physics.
El refrigerador funciona por medio de electricidad.	The fridge works by means of electricity.

- **Manner of communication or travel**

We use *por* to describe the way in which something (e.g. a person or a piece of information) has traveled.

Listen to Track 224

Me lo dijo por teléfono.	She told me by phone.
Mi paquete fue enviado por avión	My package was sent by plane.
Lo enviaré por correo.	I'll send it by/in the post.

- **On behalf of**

We use *por* when describing things done on someone's behalf.

Listen to Track 225

Llamé a Juan por ti.	I called Juan for you/on your behalf.

- **For the sake of**

Por can be used to refer to doing something for the sake/good of something/someone.

Listen to Track 226

Voy a dejar de beber por mi salud.	I'm going to quit drinking for (the sake of) my health.

But it can also be used to portray a pointless action:

Pelear por pelear.	To fight for the sake of fighting.
Lo está lavando por lavar.	He's just washing it for the sake of it.

- **In favor of**

Estar para means "to be about to." If we use *por* instead of *para*, we get a completely different phrase. *Estar por* is used to literally say you're "for" (as opposed to "against") something.

Listen to Track 227

Estoy aquí por los derechos humanos.	I'm here for human rights.

- **Yet to be done**

Another way we can use *estar* with *por* is to talk about something that has yet to be done, or something that will be done. Just put an infinitive after the *por*!

Listen to Track 228

| *El baño está por ser limpiado.* | The bathroom is yet to be cleaned. |
| *Laura está por llegar.* | Laura is yet to arrive. |

- **Location**

Por can be used to describe the general area of a location.

Listen to Track 229

| *Nick viajó por Perú.* | Nick traveled around Peru. |

Similarly, if an object moves through another object, use *por*.

| *El auto pasó por el puente.* | The car passed through the bridge. |

- **Exchange/price**

Use *por* to say that you bought something for a certain amount, or to describe swapping something for something else.

Listen to Track 230

| *Juan compró el reloj por $3,000.* | Juan bought the watch for $3,000. |
| *Te doy mis papas fritas, por tus galletas.* | I'll give you my fries for your cookies. |

- **Multiplied by**

In math, *por* is used when multiplying numbers. It translates in this case as "by."

Listen to Track 231

| *Tres por tres son nueve.* | 3 x 3 = 9 |
| *La hoja de papel mide 6 por 10 cm.* | The sheet of paper measures 6 by 10 cm. |

- **"By" in passive constructions**

Por is often used in passive constructions when we want to describe something that was done by someone. Check out these **examples:**

Listen to Track 232

| El libro fue escrito por Cervantes. | The book was written by Cervantes. |
| La mujer fue atacada por el cocodrilo. | The woman was attacked by the crocodile. |

- **To take for...**

To perceive someone or something in a certain way.

Listen to Track 233

| ¡No me tomes por idiota! | Don't take me for an idiot. |
| Lo damos por sentado. | We take him for granted. |

- **To judge by/going by**

This is a situation when you want to make a judgment based on some other information.

Listen to Track 234

| Por lo que me dijo, ... | Going by what she told me, ... |
| Por su voz, creo que estaba feliz. | Judging by his voice, I think he was happy. |

- **In search of something**

Just as in English, we can use *por* when we are going to get something.

Listen to Track 235

| Fui por mi coche. | I went for my car. |
| Marco fue a la tienda por fruta. | Marco went to the store for fruit. |

- **However much...**

We don't mean "however" in the sense of "but." We're using it in the sense of "however much X happens, Y won't happen." Check out the **examples:**

Listen to Track 236

| Por más que te quejes, no cambiará nada. | However much you complain, nothing will change. |
| Por mucho dinero que tenga, no comprará un coche nuevo. | However much money he has, he won't buy a new car. |

- **Duration**

This one is a little complicated. In some situations, *para* (in the case of the duration of something in the future), or even no preposition at all, will be preferable. But when you want to emphasize that something only lasted for a short period of time, use *por*.

Listen to Track 237

| Solo estuvo aquí por un momento. | He was only here for a moment. |

Use *por* when you want to say how long something lasted in general.

| Me quedé en el hotel por dos semanas. | I stayed in the hotel for two weeks. |
| Vi la serie por tres horas seguidas. | I watched the series for three straight hours. |

- **Gracias**

When giving thanks for something, we always use *por* not *para*.

Listen to Track 238

| Gracias por el anillo. | Thank you for the ring. |
| Muchas gracias por venir. | Thank you very much for coming. |

Workbook lesson 18: When to use "por" vs. "para"

Exercise 1: Select the correct preposition in each case choosing between "por" or "para."

1- Te felicito **por / para** tu trabajo. (Congratulations on your work.)
2- Hay que comprar comida **para / por** el sábado. (We have to buy food by Saturday.)
3- ¿**Por/ para** quién es esto? (Who is this for?)
4- No pudimos salir **para/ por** el frío. (We can't go out in the cold.)
5- Sube el volumen **por/ para** oír la música mejor. (Turn up the volume to hear the music better.)

Exercise 2: Complete the correct preposition in each case using "por" or "para."

1- Él vino ____ pedirte un favor. (He came to ask you a favor.)
2- Javier fue rechazado ____ Susana. (Javier was rejected by Susana.)
3- Tienes que haberlo escrito____ el jueves. (You must have it written by Thursday.)
4- Gracias ____ ser mi mejor amigo. (Thanks for being my best friend.)
5- Él me lo vendió ____ $50. (He sold it to me for $50.)

Exercise 3: Tick the right answer to complete the sentences.

1- Los juguetes son ____ los niños.
   a. por					b. para

2- He decidido cambiar mi departamento ____ una casa.
   a. por					b. para

3- Compré dos pantalones____ el precio de uno.
   a. por					b. para

4- Repartimos dos caramelos ____ niño.
   a. por					b. para

5- Usaré este libro____ estudiar geometría.
   a. para					b. por

Exercise 4: Translate the following sentences from Spanish to English.

1- Mi mamá cambió su vehículo por uno nuevo.
   _____

2- Tengo la mañana para caminar.
   _____

3- El libro estaba por aquí.
   _____

4- Hago ejercicio por las mañanas.
   _____

5- No sirve para nada.
   _____

Exercise 5: Complete these sentences with "por" or "para."

1- Pelear _____ pelear. (Fighting for fighting's sake.)
2- Estoy _____ los derechos humanos. (I am for human rights.)
3- El baño está _____ ser limpiado. (The bathroom will be cleaned.)
4- Lizeth está _____ llegar. (Lizeth is coming.)
5- Karen viajó _____ la Guyana. (Karen traveled through Guyana.)

Exercise 6: Complete the paragraph with "por" or "para."

El viernes mis amigos y yo nos iremos 1. _____ Texas 2. _____ visitar a nuestro amigo Tom. Vamos allá 3. _____ descansar también. No tenemos mucho dinero, 4. _____ consiguiente optamos 5. _____ ir en coche.

Answers:

Exercise 1

1/ Te felicito por tu trabajo. 2/ Hay que comprar comida para el sábado. 3/ ¿Para quién es esto? 4/ No podemos salir por el frío. 5/ Sube el volumen para oír la música mejor.

Exercise 2

1/ Él vino para pedirte un favor. 2/ Javier fue rechazado por Susana. 3/ Tienes que haberlo escrito para el jueves. 4/ Gracias por ser mi mejor amigo. 5/ Él me lo vendió por $50.

Exercise 3

1/ para 2/ por 3/ por 4/ por 5/ para

Exercise 4

1/ My mom traded her vehicle for a new one. 2/ I have the morning to walk. 3/ The book was by here. 4/ I do sport in the mornings. 5/ It's useless.

Exercise 5

1/ Pelear por pelear. 2/ Estoy por los derechos humanos. 3/ El baño está por ser limpiado. 4/ Lizeth está por llegar. 5/ Karen viajó por la Guyana.

Exercise 6

El viernes mis amigos y yo nos iremos para Texas para visitar a nuestro amigo Tom. Vamos allá para descansar también. No tenemos mucho dinero, por consiguiente, optamos por ir en coche.

Lesson 19: Perfect tense – Tiempo perfecto

Being able to conjugate verbs in the perfect tense is a great skill to have, as it helps you to describe things that have occurred in the past. All you need to know is how to conjugate one verb (*haber*), and how to form past participles. In today's lesson, we'll learn how to do just that.

What is the perfect tense?

You might hear lots of different names for this tense, like "present perfect," "perfect indicative," or "*pretérito perfecto compuesto.*" Don't be put off by these names; they all mean the same thing, a tense we'll call "the perfect tense" for simplicity!

We use the perfect tense to describe something that has happened in the not-too-distant past.

As we said before, it's more commonly used in Spain than in Mexico or Latin America, just as it's more common in the UK than the USA. Here's a table to demonstrate the difference between the perfect tense and the preterite (which is a completely different past tense).

Perfect tense	Preterite tense
I have eaten dinner (already tonight).	I ate dinner (yesterday).
What have you been doing (today, before you came here)?	What did you do (at a specific point in the distant past)?
I've been skating (today).	I went skating (at a specific point in the distant past).
It has been a pleasure to meet you (today).	It was a pleasure to meet her (last week).
I think it has rained (recently, because it's wet now).	I think it rained (last week, but it may well be dry today).

With practice, it will soon become clear when to use which tense. Basically, if you want to say, "I have ...-ed," then you'll need the perfect tense.

How to form it

The perfect tense is pretty easy to form, as it's made of two simple parts: *haber* + past participle.

Haber

This verb means "to have" when it's used in certain tenses, including the perfect tense (not to be confused with *tener*, which means "to have" in pretty much all *other* situations).

Listen to Track 239

Here is the conjugation of *haber* that you'll need:

Yo	he	I have
Tú	has	You have
Él/ella	ha	He/she/it has
Usted		You (formal) have
Nosotros	hemos	We have
Ustedes	han	You (you plural) have
Ellos/ellas	han	They have

Top tip: Remember that in Spanish, the 'h" is silent.

For the perfect tense, this is the only verb you need to know how to conjugate! The past participles don't actually need to be conjugated...

Past participles

The past participle in English is the -ed form version of a regular verb, e.g. knitted, played, worked.

Regular formation

The normal formation of past participles is super simple. You take the verb in the infinitive, then:

For *-ar* verbs, remove the *-ar* then add *-ado*.

For *-er* and *-ir* verbs, remove the *-er* or *-ir* then add *-ido*.

For example:

Listen to Track 240

to play:	*jugar* →	*jugar* →	*jug + ado*	→	*jugado*
to love:	*amar* →	*amar* →	*am + ado*	→	*amado*
to eat:	*comer* →	*comer* →	*com + ido*	→	*comido*
to drink:	*beber* →	*beber* →	*beb + ido*	→	*bebido*
to live:	*vivir* →	*vivir* →	*viv + ido*	→	*vivido*

Irregular past participles

Surprisingly, the normally very awkward verbs *ir*, *ser*, and *estar* actually form their past participles in the regular way!

Listen to Track 241

to go:	ir	→	-~~ir~~	→	- + ido	→	ido
to be:	ser	→	s~~er~~	→	s + ido	→	sido
to be:	estar	→	est~~ar~~	→	est + ado	→	estado

For example:

Listen to Track 242

- Yo no **he ido** a Japón. (I have not been to Japan)
- Nosotros siempre **hemos sido** sus favoritos. (We have always been his favorites)
- Él **ha estado** en tu situación. (He has been in your situation)

However, as this is Spanish, there'll always be some irregular ones around. The following have irregular past participles which need to be learned.

Top tip: You might start to spot patterns for how the irregular ones are formed, e.g. things that end in *-cubrir* (*cubrir*, *descubrir*, etc.) have past participles that end in *-cubierto* (*cubierto*, *descubierto*, etc.).

Listen to Track 243

Infinitive	Past participle	English
Abrir	abierto	opened
Cubrir	cubierto	covered
Decir	dicho	said
Descubrir	descubierto	discovered
Escribir	escrito	written
Freír	frito	fried
Hacer	hecho	done/made
Imprimir	impreso	printed
Morir	muerto	died
Poner	puesto	put
Resolver	resuelto	resolved

Romper	roto	broken
Satisfacer	satisfecho	satisfied
Ver	visto	seen
Volver	vuelto	returned

For example:

Listen to Track 244

- ¿Quién **ha abierto** la puerta? (Who has opened the door?)
- Nadie **ha escrito** nada. (Nobody has written anything.)
- Mi perro no **ha roto** ni un plato. (My dog hasn't even broken a single plate.)

Triggers

A good general rule is that if you're talking about something that's happened in "this [time period]," e.g. "today" (this day), "this morning," "this week," "this month," "this year," then you'll need the perfect tense. It's also useful to recognize other phrases that trigger the perfect tense. Here are some common ones to look out for!

Listen to Track 245

Hoy	today
Ya	already
Recientemente	recently
X veces	x times
Todavía	still
Nunca/jamás	never

BONUS LESSON: The Pluperfect Tense

If you got all of that, you might want to think about the pluperfect tense. Instead of talking about things that *have happened* (before now), it allows you to describe things that *had already happened* before a point of time in the past.

It's formed in almost the same way as the perfect tense, except that *haber* is conjugated in the imperfect (another type of past tense):

Listen to Track 246

Yo	había	I had
Tú	habías	You had
Él/ella	había	He/she/it had
Usted		You (formal) had
Nosotros	habíamos	We had
Ustedes	habían	You (you plural) had
Ellos/ellas	habían	They had

To sum up ...

Listen to Track 247

Perfect:	*He* + past participle (*He comido*)	I have + past participle (I have eaten)
Pluperfect:	*Había* + past participle (*Había comido*)	I had + past participle (I had eaten)

Workbook Lesson 19: Perfect tense – Tiempo perfecto

Exercise 1: Use the perfect tense to complete the sentences. Use "haber" + the verb in the past participle.

1- Este verano _____ _____ (estar) en Alaska. (This summer we went to Alaska.)
2- Este año _____ _____ (llover) mucho. (This year it has rained a lot.)
3- Se _____ _____ (despertar) a las 10. (He woke up at 10.)
4- ¿Tú _____ _____ (leer) algo interesante últimamente? (Have you read anything interesting lately?)
5- Hoy nosotras _____ _____ (comer) ceviche. (Today we have eaten ceviche.)

Exercise 2: Translate the following sentences from Spanish to English.

1- ¿Tú has visto a Eduardo?
   _____

2- ¿Qué han hecho ustedes este verano?
   _____

3- Hoy hemos trabajado cerca de 10 horas.
   _____

4- Él ha jugado fútbol.
   _____

5- Ella ha enviado unos correos.
   _____

Exercise 3: Choose the right answer.

1- He _____ una vida intensa.
   a. tenido   b. teniado

2- Yo _____ actriz de Hollywood.
   a. he sido   b. has sido

3- Ella _____ por todo el mundo.
   a. ha viajado   b. has viajado

4- Nosotros _____ en una fábrica.
   a. hemos trabajado b. han trabajado

5- Pedro nunca _____ de México.
   a. ha salido   b. han salido

Exercise 4: Use the perfect tense to complete the sentences. Use "haber" + the verb in the past participle.

1- Pedro _____ _____ (estar) en Uruguay. (Pedro has been to Uruguay.)
2- Ellos _____ _____ (tener) cinco hijos. (They have had five children.)
3- Yo _____ _____ (conocer) personajes famosos. (I have met famous celebrities.)
4- ¿Tú _____ _____ (comer) paella alguna vez? (Have you ever eaten paella?)
5- Nosotras nunca _____ _____ (tomar) tequila. (We have never had tequila.)

Exercise 5: Form phrases by pairing elements from the two columns.

Example: No he podido llamar porque he trabajado mucho todo el día.

1- No puedo entrar a la casa	1- Trabajar mucho todo el día
2- Juana no ve bien	2- Olvidar la cartera
3- No puedo pagar	3- Perder las llaves
4- Están agotadas	4- Romper los lentes
5- No he podido llamar	5- Tener tiempo

Answers:

Exercise 1

1/ Este verano hemos estado en Alaska. 2/ Este año ha llovido mucho. 3/ Se ha despertado a las 10. 4/ ¿Tú has leído algo interesante últimamente? 5/ Hoy nosotras hemos comido ceviche.

Exercise 2

1/ Have you seen Eduardo? 2/ What have you done this summer? 3/ Today we have worked about 10 hours. 4/ He has been playing soccer. 5/ She has sent some emails.

Exercise 3

1/ tenido 2/ he sido 3/ ha viajado 4/ hemos trabajado 5/ ha salido

Exercise 4

1/ Pedro ha estado en Uruguay. 2/ Ellos han tenido cinco hijos. 3/ Yo he conocido personajes famosos. 4/ ¿Tú has comido alguna vez paella? 5/ Nosotras nunca hemos tomado tequila.

Exercise 5

1/ No puedo entrar a la casa porque he perdido las llaves. 2/ Juana no ve bien porque ha roto los lentes. 3/ No puedo pagar porque he olvidado la cartera. 4/ Están agotadas porque han trabajado mucho todo el día. 5/ No he podido llamar porque no he tenido tiempo.

Lesson 20: Possessives – Posesivos

What are possessives?

Possessives are used to describe who owns (or possesses) something. In English, these are "my," "your," "our" and so on.

We can split Spanish possessives into three groups:

- Possessive adjectives - short form
- Possessive adjectives - longer form
- Possessive pronouns

Let's look at them in turn.

Possessive Adjectives—Short Form

The short version is the most common form of possessive adjective, and you just stick it in front of the noun.

A really important thing to remember is that the possessive adjective has to agree in number and gender with the thing that's possessed, not the person possessing it. We'll show you some examples later.

Here are the short form possessive adjectives:

Listen to Track 248

Mi(s)	My
Tu(s)	Your (familiar singular)
Su(s)	His/her/its/your (formal singular)
Nuestro(s)/nuestra(s)	Our
Su(s)	Their/Your (you plural)

It helps to look at the words in context, and get a bit of practice. Here are some example sentences to start you off:

Listen to Track 249

Estoy buscando mi llave.	I'm looking for my key.
Estoy buscando mis llaves.	I'm looking for my keys.
Toma tu libro.	Take your book.
Toma tus libros.	Take your books.
Alejandra ha perdido sus lentes.	Alejandra has lost her glasses.
Señora, ¿dónde está su perro?	Madam, where is your dog? (formal)
Nosotros/nosotras estamos en nuestro país.	We are in our country.
Nosotros/nosotras estamos en nuestra casa.	We are in our house.
Estamos con nuestros primos.	We are with our cousins. (male/mixed)
Estamos con nuestras primas.	We are with our cousins. (female)
¿Quién es su padre?	Who is your father? (formal)
¿Dónde está su madre?	Where is your mother? (formal)
¿Quiénes son sus padres?	Who are your parents? (formal)
¿Dónde están sus hermanas?	Where are your sisters? (formal)
Soy su hija.	I'm their daughter.
Soy su mesero.	I'm your waiter. (you plural)

Possessive Adjectives—Longer Form

These mean pretty much the same as the short form adjectives, but they help to emphasize who is possessing, rather than focusing on the possessed object. We place them after the noun being possessed.

This time, it's not just *nuestro* that has to agree in gender. All the forms have to agree in gender AND number with the thing being possessed.

Listen to Track 250

mío(s)/mía(s)	My
tuyo(s)/tuya(s)	Your (familiar singular)
suyo(s)/suya(s)	His/her
	Your (formal singular)
nuestro(s)/nuestra(s)	Our
suyo(s)/suya(s)	Their
	Your (plural)

As you look at the following examples, remember that *suyo(s)/suya(s)* can have various meanings. Context will usually make things clear.

Listen to Track 251

¡Dios mío!	My God!
Veo a dos hermanos míos por ahí.	I see two of my brothers over there.
No llores, hija mía.	Don't cry, my dear (daughter).
Paula y Claudia son amigas mías.	Paula and Claudia are friends of mine.
Fue un error tuyo.	It was a mistake of yours (it was your mistake).
Fueron errores tuyos.	They were mistakes of yours.
Fue una idea tuya.	It was an idea of yours (it was your idea).
Fueron ideas tuyas.	They were ideas of yours.
Necesito encontrar a Pablo. Tengo que devolverle un documento suyo.	I need to find Pablo. I have to give back a document of his.
Necesito encontrar a Pablo. Tengo que devolverle unos documentos suyos.	I need to find Pablo. I have to give back some documents of his.
Necesito encontrar a Pablo. Tengo que devolverle una corbata suya.	I need to find Pablo. I have to give back a necktie of his.
Necesito encontrar a Pablo. Tengo que devolverle unas corbatas suyas.	I need to find Pablo. I have to give back some neckties of his.
¿Es un conocido suyo?	Is he an acquaintance of yours? (formal singular)
¿Son conocidos suyos?	Are they acquaintances of yours?
¿Es una amiga suya?	Is she a friend (female) of yours?
¿Son amigas suyas?	Are they friends (females) of yours?
Es un traje nuestro.	It's a suit of ours.
Son trajes nuestros.	They're suits of ours.

Es hermana nuestra.	She's a sister of ours.
Son algunas de nuestras hermanas.	They're some of our sisters.
Chicos, es un logro suyo.	Guys, it's an achievement of yours. (familiar plural)
Chicos, todos son logros suyos.	Guys, they're all achievements of yours.
Chicos, ¿fue esto una broma suya?	Guys, was this a prank of yours?
Chicos, ¿fueron bromas suyas?	Guys, were they pranks of yours?
Juan es un compañero suyo.	Juan is a colleague of theirs.
Juan y Pol son compañeros suyos.	Juan and Pol are colleagues of theirs.
Ana es prima suya.	Ana is a cousin (female) of theirs.
Ana y Andrea son primas suyas.	Ana and Andrea are cousins (female) of theirs.
Señores, ya hemos escuchado un discurso suyo.	Gentlemen, we have already heard a speech of yours. (you plural)
Señores, ya hemos escuchado algunos discursos suyos.	Gentlemen, we have already heard speeches of yours.
Señores, leí una carta suya.	Gentlemen, I read a letter of yours.
Señores, leí unas cartas suyas.	Gentlemen, I read some letters of yours.

Possessive Pronouns

Sometimes the longer form is used with the definite article (*el/la/los/las*).

The difference is that in these cases, the possessive is acting as a pronoun, meaning that it replaces the noun rather than modifying it.

The possessive pronouns are the same as the longer form possessives as mentioned above. Here's a reminder:

Listen to Track 252

Mío(s)/Mía(s)	Mine
Tuyo(s)/Tuya(s)	Yours (familiar)
Suyo(s)/Suya(s)	His/hers/yours (formal)
Nuestro(s)/Nuestra(s)	Ours
Suyo(s)/Suya(s)	Theirs/yours (plural)

Again, remember that *suyo(s)/suya(s)* can have various meanings.

Listen to Track 253-254

Este plátano es el mío.	This banana is mine (my one).
Estos plátanos son los míos.	These bananas are mine (my ones).
Esa fresa es la mía.	That strawberry is mine (my one).
Esas fresas son las mías.	Those strawberries are mine (my ones).
Vi el tuyo.	I saw yours (your one).
Vi los tuyos.	I saw yours (your ones).
Vi la tuya.	I saw yours (your one).
Vi las tuyas.	I saw yours (your ones).
¿Cuál perro?	Which dog?
—El suyo.	Hers (her one).
¿Cuáles perros?	Which dogs?
—Los suyos.	Hers (her ones).
¿De cuál falda hablamos?	Which skirt are we talking about?
—(De) La suya.	Hers (her one).
¿De cuáles faldas hablamos?	Which skirts are we talking about?
—(De) Las suyas.	Hers (her ones).
Este libro es el suyo.	This book is yours (formal singular) (your one).
Estos libros son los suyos.	These books are yours (your ones).
Creo que esta bebida es la suya.	I think this drink is yours (your one).
Creo que estas bebidas son las suyas.	I think these drinks are yours (your ones).

Listen to Track 254

Ese es el nuestro.	This one is ours (our one).
Esos son los nuestros.	These ones are ours (our ones).
Esa es la nuestra.	That one is ours (our one).
Esas son las nuestras.	Those ones are ours (our ones).
Mi deseo es aprender. ¿Y el suyo?	My desire is to learn. And yours (familiar plural) (your one)?
Mis planes son claros. ¿Y los suyos?	My plans are clear. And yours (your ones)?
La idea de ellos es impresionante. ¿Cuál es la suya?	Their idea is impressive. What is yours (your one)?
Las ideas de ellos son impresionantes. ¿Ya tienen las suyas?	Their ideas are impressive. Do you have yours (your ones) yet?

Juan y Ángel viven en la esquina. El edificio café es el suyo.	Juan and Ángel live on the corner. The brown building is theirs (their one).
Juan y Ángel se estacionaron ahí. Los coches azules son los suyos.	Juan and Ángel parked over there. The blue cars are theirs (their ones).
Juan y Ángel viven en la esquina. La casa verde es la suya.	Juan and Ángel live on the corner. The green house is theirs (their one).
Juan y Ángel se estacionaron ahí. Las motos negras son las suyas.	Juan and Ángel parked over there. The black motorcycles are theirs (their ones).
Señores y señoras, este mesero es el suyo.	Ladies and gentlemen, this waiter is yours (your one).
Señores y señoras, estos meseros son los suyos.	Ladies and gentlemen, these waiters are yours (your ones).
Señores y señoras, esta mesa es la suya.	Ladies and gentlemen, this table is yours (your one).
Señores y señoras, estas mesas son las suyas.	Ladies and gentlemen, these tables are yours (your ones).

And something else...

You can also use a long form possessive with *lo* to refer to some unnamed business, or to say that you're in your element:

Listen to Track 255

¡Mi novio sabe de lo nuestro!	My boyfriend knows about us!
Lo suyo es fascinante.	That stuff with you guys is fascinating.
Eso es lo mío.	This is my thing./I'm in my element.

We have lots of phrases in English where we use a possessive with body parts. In Spanish, we actually don't use the possessive in these cases:

Listen to Track 256

Me duele la cabeza.	My head hurts.
Dame la mano.	Give me your hand.
Cierra la boca.	Shut your mouth.

Workbook Lesson 20: Possessives – Posesivos

Exercise 1: Complete the phrases with possessive adjectives.

1- ¿Cuál es _____ color preferido? (What is your favorite color?)
2- Mi hermano y yo jugamos mucho al tenis, es _____ deporte favorito. (My brother and I play tennis a lot. It's our favorite sport.)
3- La señora Marta y _____ hijos son muy agradables. (Mrs. Martha and her children are very nice.)
4- Anoche fui al cine con _____ padre y _____ hermanos. (Last night I went to the movies with my father and my brothers.)
5- Juan, Pedro, ¿dónde están _____ libros? (Juan, Pedro, where are your books?)

Exercise 2: Translate the following sentences from Spanish to English.

1- Rodrigo trabaja con su padre.
   _____

2- Su abuela tiene 86 años.
   _____

3- Dame tu chaqueta.
   _____

4- ¿Quién es tu profesor?
   _____

5- Abel es su mujer.
   _____

Exercise 3: Complete sentences as in the example.

Example: ¿De quién es este libro? Es mío.

1- ¿De quién son estas llaves? Son _____. (Whose keys are these? They are mine.)
2- ¿Son _____ estas maletas? (Are these suitcases yours?)
3- ¿De quién son estos CDs? Son _____. (Whose are these CDs? They're ours.)
4- ¿Es _____ este reloj? (Is this watch yours?)
5- ¿De quién es este paraguas? Es _____. (Whose umbrella is this? It's yours.)

Exercise 4: Tick the right answer.

1- ¿Es ese su coche? No ____ es más grande.
   a. el mío   b. mío

2- Este abrigo no es de Pedro. ____ es negro.
   a. El suyo   b. Tuyo

3- ¿Ese es nuestro profesor? No____ es más joven.
   a. el suyo   b. el nuestro

4- Mi profesora es peruana. ____ es colombiana.
   a. La mía   b. La mío

5- Un amigo____ es pintor.
   a. mío   b. el mío

Exercise 5: Sort the following words to create sentences.

1- mi coche/ es / el tuyo /caro /pero / es más. (My car is expensive, but yours is more.)
   _____

2- ha / perdido /equipo / nuestro. (Our team has lost.)
   _____

3- abuelos / se llaman / tus / Pedro y Ana. (Your grandparents are called Peter and Ana.)
   _____

4- hijos / son / mis / muy inteligentes. (My children are very intelligent.)
   _____

5- perro/ tu / es / muy cariñoso. (Your dog is very sweet.)
   _____

Exercise 6: Complete the statements below using possessive adjectives.

¿Quieres saber algo de ____ familia? Pues mira, ____ familia no es muy grande, pero vivimos en diferentes ciudades de México. ____ padres están jubilados y viven en ____ casa que está en Guadalajara. ____ hermana se llama Claudia y ella y ____ marido Fernando viven en Cancún. (You want to know about our family? Look, my family's not very big, but we live in different cities in Mexico. My parents are retired and live in their home in Guadalajara. My sister's name is Claudia, and she and her husband Fernando live in Cancún.)

Answers:

Exercise 1

1/ ¿Cuál es tu color preferido? 2/ Mi hermano y yo jugamos mucho al tenis, es nuestro deporte favorito. 3/ La señora Marta y sus hijos son muy agradables. 4/ Anoche fui al cine con mi padre y mis hermanos. 5/ Juan, Pedro, ¿dónde están sus libros?

Exercise 2

1/ Rodrigo works with his father. 2/ His grandmother is 86 years old. 3/ Give me your jacket. 4/ Who's your teacher? 5/ Abel is his wife.

Exercise 3

1/ ¿De quién son estas llaves? Son mías. 2/ ¿Son suyas estas maletas? 3/ ¿De quién son estos CDs? Son nuestros. 4/ ¿Es tuyo este reloj? 5/ ¿De quién es este paraguas? Es suyo.

Exercise 4

1/ el mío 2/ el suyo 3/ el nuestro 4/ la mía 5/ mío

Exercise 5

1/ Mi coche es caro, pero el tuyo es más. 2/ Nuestro equipo ha perdido. 3/ Tus abuelos se llaman Pedro y Ana. 4/ Mis hijos son muy inteligentes. 5/ Tu perro es muy cariñoso.

Exercise 6

¿Quieres saber algo de nuestra familia? Pues mira, mi familia no es muy grande, pero vivimos en diferentes ciudades de México. Mis padres están jubilados y viven en su casa que está en Guadalajara, Jalisco. Mi hermana se llama Claudia y ella y su marido Fernando viven en Cancún.

Lesson 21: Demonstrative adjectives and demonstrative pronouns – Adjetivos demostrativos y pronombres demostrativos

Demonstrative adjectives and demonstrative pronouns are not the same thing, so let's start by looking at the adjectives and then move on to the pronouns.

What is a demonstrative adjective?

Demonstrative adjectives *demonstrate* which thing is being talked about. Adjectives are words that modify nouns. So basically, a demonstrative adjective is a word that you put before a noun, and it specifies which noun you're referring to if there's any ambiguity (e.g. "*this* egg" vs. "*that* egg").

In English, we distinguish between "this" and "that." In Spanish, there's one additional level. Spanish-speakers differentiate between "that which isn't right next to me but isn't too far away" and "that all the way over there." In other words, there are two different versions of "that" depending on how far away the object is!

So, the Spanish demonstrative adjectives are these:

<u>*Listen to Track 257*</u>

Este ___	This ___ (masculine)
Esta ___	This ___ (feminine)
Estos ___	These ___ (masculine plural)
Estas ___	These ___ (feminine plural)
Ese ___	That ___ (masculine)
Esa ___	That ___ (feminine)
Esos ___	Those ___ (masculine plural)
Esas ___	Those ___ (feminine plural)
Aquel ___	That ___ over there (masculine)
Aquella ___	That ___ over there (feminine)
Aquellos ___	Those ___ over there (masculine plural)
Aquellas ___	Those ___ over there (feminine plural)

How they work

They're adjectives and we put them before nouns, just like in English. The demonstrative adjective that you use has to agree in gender (masculine or feminine) and number (singular or plural) with the noun it's modifying. We've listed all the gender and number options above.

Lesson 21: Demonstrative adjectives and demonstrative pronouns – Adjetivos demostrativos y pronombres demostrativos

Here are some examples for you to read, to give you some context and help you understand how to use demonstrative adjectives.

Listen to Track 258

Este anillo es de oro.	This ring is made of gold.
Compré este libro ayer.	I bought this book yesterday.
Esta mañana fui al mercado.	This morning I went to the market.
Me encanta esta falda.	I love this skirt.
Estos perros son míos.	These dogs are mine.
Vendrá uno de estos días.	He will come one of these days.
Estas máquinas están rotas.	These machines are broken.
Quiero comprar estas chaquetas.	I want to buy these jackets.

Ese camión va al centro.	That bus goes to the city center.
Dame ese lápiz.	Pass me that pen.
Esa mochila es de Beatriz.	That backpack belongs to Beatriz.
Me gusta esa foto.	I like that photo.
Esos zapatos son de muy buena calidad.	Those shoes are really good quality.
¿Estás cómodo usando esos pantalones?	Are you comfortable wearing those jeans?
Esas arañas me dan miedo.	Those spiders frighten me.
La señora robó una de esas manzanas.	The lady stole one of those apples.

Listen to Track 259

Aquel edificio es donde trabaja mi madre.	That office over there is where my mother works.
Me gusta mucho aquel chico.	I really like that guy over there.
Aquella chica no deja de mirarme.	That girl over there won't stop staring at me.
No nos conocíamos en aquella época.	We didn't know each other in those days (far away in time, in the distant past).
Aquellos hombres son artistas.	Those men over there are artists.
No he estado en aquellos países.	I haven't been to those (faraway) countries.
Aquellas mujeres son muy inteligentes.	Those women over there are very intelligent.
Me gustaría caminar por aquellas montañas.	I'd like to walk around those mountains over there.

For native English speakers, correctly differentiating between *ese* (that) and *aquel* (that over there) can take a while to master. Here are some sentences that make use of "this," "that," and "that over there" so you can see the difference.

Listen to Track 260

Carlos, no me basta esta hoja de papel. ¿Me pasas ese cuaderno? Si no, mejor voy a usar aquella computadora.	Carlos, this sheet of paper isn't big enough. Would you pass me that notebook? Otherwise, I'll go use that computer.
Rafael quiere entrar en esta iglesia y Nerea quiere visitar ese museo en la próxima calle. Yo quiero caminar hasta aquella torre afuera del pueblo.	Rafael wants to go into this church, and Nerea wants to visit that museum in the next street. I want to walk to that tower outside the village.
Este hombre es mi marido, ese señor a tu lado es su padre y aquellos niños jugando afuera son nuestros hijos.	This man is my husband. That man next to you is his father. Those children playing outside are our children.
No toques esta pluma, es mía. Ese lápiz es tuyo, o puedes buscar aquellos colores que te compró mamá ayer.	Don't touch this pen. It's mine. That pencil is yours. Or you can look for those crayons that Mommy bought you yesterday.

What is a demonstrative pronoun?

Now let's move on to pronouns. As we said earlier, demonstratives *demonstrate* which thing someone is talking about. Pronouns are words that replace nouns. So basically, a demonstrative pronoun is a word that you use instead of a noun, and it specifies which noun you're referring to.

Demonstrative pronouns are useful when we don't have to give as much context. If we already know we're talking about cars, we don't need to say "this car" and "that car." Instead, we can just say "this" and "that."

So, the Spanish demonstrative pronouns are these:

Listen to Track 261

Este	This (masculine)
Esta	This (feminine)
Estos	These (masculine plural)
Estas	These (feminine plural)
Ese	That (masculine)
Esa	That (feminine)

Esos	Those (masculine plural)
Esas	Those (feminine plural)
Aquel	That (masculine)
Aquella	That (feminine)
Aquellos	Those (masculine plural)
Aquellas	Those (feminine plural)

An important note on spelling...

Until recently, demonstrative pronouns (except the neuter ones mentioned below) had an accent on them. This was to differentiate between demonstrative adjectives and demonstrative pronouns, and you used to have to remember which ones took accents. It looked something like this:

Listen to Track 262

Me gusta esta casa. (I like this house.) vs. *Me gusta ésta.* (I like this one.)

Aquel gato es mío. (That cat is mine.) vs. *Aquél es mío.* (That one is mine.)

It's good for you to be aware of this, because a lot of what you read will still use the old rules. But the new rule leaves out the accents altogether!

How they work

Because they're pronouns, they're used to replace nouns. The demonstrative pronoun that you choose has to agree in gender and number with the noun it's replacing. And don't forget to differentiate between "that" and "that over there"!

Demonstrative pronouns are a little different from demonstrative adjectives, because as well as masculine and feminine forms, you have a kind of genderless form, called the "neuter" form.

It's used when we're not referring to a particular noun. It can be used to refer to ideas, statements, or sometimes objects, but not living things – if we're talking about a person or animal, we need to figure out its gender and use the corresponding masculine or feminine pronoun.

The neuter ones:

Listen to Track 263

Esto	This
Eso	That
Aquello	That (more distant)

Examples

Look through these sentences and see if they make sense!

Listen to Track 264

Este es mi coche.	This one is my car.
Dame otra pluma. Esta no escribe.	Give me another pen. This one doesn't work.
Esta es mi falda favorita.	This skirt is my favorite one.
En una oficina como esta, hay que trabajar duro.	In an office like this one, you have to work hard.
Estos dos son los míos.	These two are mine.
A ver si estos funcionan.	Let's see if these work.
Estas son mejores que aquellas.	These are better than those over there.
Me encantaría tener calificaciones como estas.	I'd love to have grades like these.
(NEUTER) *Esto me hace feliz.*	This (situation/environment) makes me happy.
(NEUTER) *¿Quién ha hecho esto?*	Who's done this?

Ese es mejor que este.	That one is better than this one.
No me gusta este hombre. Prefiero ese.	I don't like this man. I prefer that one.
Esa es la mía.	That one is mine.
No quiero esta vela. Quiero esa, la rosa.	I don't want this candle. I want that one, the pink one.
Esos son los mejores.	Those ones are the best.
Nos gustan estos libros, pero nos gustan también esos.	We like these books, but we also like those.
Esas sí que son valientes.	Now those ones—they're brave.
¿Que cuáles flores me gustan? ¡Me encantan esas!	Which flowers do I like? I love those ones!
(NEUTER) *¡Eso es, campeón! ¡Muy bien!*	That's it, buddy! Well done!
(NEUTER) *Quiero que pare todo eso.*	I want all that to stop.

Lesson 21: Demonstrative adjectives and demonstrative pronouns – Adjetivos demostrativos y pronombres demostrativos

Listen to Track 265

Aquel sería el mejor.	That one over there would be the best one.
No me gusta este traje. Voy a comprar aquel.	I don't like this suit. I'm going to buy that one over there.
Aquella fue la época más violenta.	That was the most violent era.
¿Cuál? *—Aquella.*	Which one? —That one.
Aquellos son tuyos. Esos son míos.	Those ones over there are yours. Those (a bit closer) are mine.
¿Aquellos son tus zapatos?	Are those your shoes?
Aquellas viven fuera de la ciudad.	Those ones live outside the city.
Mis películas favoritas son aquellas con actores poco conocidos.	My favorite movies are those with unknown actors.
(NEUTRO) Aquello es lo que te espera.	That's what awaits you.
(NEUTRO) No me meto en todo aquello.	I'm not getting involved in all that.

¡Muy bien!

Hopefully this lesson has shown you the difference between adjectives and pronouns and taught you how to use the demonstrative forms of each. Try and spot them when you're reading in Spanish and think about whether they're adjectives or pronouns.

Workbook lesson 21: Demonstrative adjectives and demonstrative pronouns – Adjetivos demostrativos y pronombres demostrativos

Exercise 1: Complete the phrases with demonstrative pronouns or adjectives.

1- _____ chica es amiga de Ana. (That girl is Ana's friend.)
2- _____ zapatos son muy caros. (These shoes are very expensive.)
3- _____ es Juan, mi novio. (This is John, my boyfriend.)
4- ¿De quién es _____? (Whose is that?)

Exercise 2: Complete the sentences as in the example.

Example: ¿De quién es ___ libro?: – ¿De quién es este libro? (Whose book is this?)

1- Me gusta mucho _____ (I really like this restaurant.)
2- _____ vaso está sucio. (This glass is dirty.)
3- ¿Conoces a _____ chico? (You know this guy?)
4- Mira, _____ es el padre de Carlos. (Look, that's Charles' father.)
5- ¿A dónde va _____ amion? (Where does this bus go?)

Exercise 3: Tick the right answer.

1- _____ verano vamos a ir a París.
   a. Este   b. Estos

2- Nací en 1989. _____ mismo año nació mi primo.
   a. Ese   b. Este

3- ¿Qué haces _____ noche?
   a. esa   b. esta

4- _____ mes ha sido fabuloso.
   a. Este   b. Aquel

5- _____ tarde tengo un examen.
   a. Esta   b. Esa

Lesson 21: Demonstrative adjectives and demonstrative pronouns – Adjetivos demostrativos y pronombres demostrativos

Exercise 4: Complete sentences as in the example. Use the following demonstratives: *este, estos, eso, esos, aquellos.*

1- Mi amigo Juan dice que _____ bar es el mejor de la ciudad. (My friend Juan says this bar is the best in the city.)

2- ¿Ustedes conocen a _____ chicas? Son hermosas. (You know those girls? They are beautiful.)

3- _____ es la casa de Ramón, la blanca. (That's Ramon's house, the white one.)

4- ¿Cuánto cuesta _____ moto? (How much is this bike?)

5- _____ día llovió sin parar. (That day it rained non-stop.)

Exercise 5: Complete the following dialogue with the corresponding demonstrative pronouns.

_____ es mi familia. Mi madre se llama Rebeca y mi papá Alberto. Tengo dos hermanos. _____ que está sentado se llama David, y el que _____ jugando es el menor, Pedro. _____ que están en el jardín son mis primos Diego y Camila. _____ que están en el patio son nuestros perros, Lancer y Claudio. Bueno, _____ es toda mi familia. ¡Que tengas un buen día!

(This is my family. My mother's name is Rebecca and my dad is Alberto. I have two brothers. This one sitting here is called David. And that one playing is the younger one, Peter. Those in the garden are my cousins, Diego and Camila. Those in the yard are our dogs, Lancer and Claudio. Well this is my whole family. Have a good day!)

Exercise 6: Translate the following sentences from Spanish to English.

1- Estas camisas cuestan 30 dólares.
   _____

2- ¿Cómo está esa pizza? Deliciosa.
   _____

3- ¿Hay alguien en esa casa?
   _____

4- ¿Quieres algo de aquella tienda?
   _____

5- Esas son las nuevas estudiantes.
   _____

Answers:

Exercise 1

1/ Esa chica es amiga de Ana. 2/ Estos zapatos son muy caros. 3/ Este es Juan, mi novio. 4/ ¿De quién es eso?

Exercise 2

1/ Me gusta mucho este restaurante. 2/ Este vaso está sucio. 3/ ¿Conoces a ese chico? 4/ Mira, ese es el padre de Carlos. 5/ ¿A dónde va este camión?

Exercise 3

1/ Este verano vamos a ir a París. 2/ Nací en 1989. Ese mismo año nació mi primo. 3/ ¿Qué haces esta noche? 4/ Este mes ha sido fabuloso. 5/ Esta tarde tengo un examen.

Exercise 4

1/ Mi amigo Juan dice que este bar es el mejor de la ciudad.
2/ ¿Ustedes conocen a esas chicas? Son hermosas. 3/ Esa es la casa de Ramón, la blanca. 4/ ¿Cuánto cuesta esta moto? 5/ Aquel día llovió sin parar.

Exercise 5

Esta es mi familia. Mi madre se llama Rebeca y mi papá Alberto. Tengo dos hermanos. Ese que está sentado se llama David y el que está jugando es el menor, Pedro. Aquellos que están en el jardín son mis primos Diego y Camila. Esos que están en el patio son nuestros perros, Lancer y Claudio. Bueno, esta es toda mi familia. ¡Que tengas un buen día!

Exercise 6

1/ These shirts cost $30. 2/ How is that pizza? Delicious. 3/ Is anyone in that house? 4/ Do you want anything from that store? 5/ Those are the new students.

Lesson 22: Making comparisons – Hacer comparaciones

In this lesson, we'll look at comparatives and superlatives, and some handy phrases that can be slipped into conversation or writing!

A comparative compares two things, while a superlative compares three or more things, including sometimes all of a particular thing that exists.

For example:

Adjective	Comparative	Superlative
bright	brighter	brightest
happy	happier	happiest
expensive	more expensive	most expensive

Comparatives

Let's start with comparatives – those are the words which often end in -er in English. We need to know how to say that A is "more + adjective" or "less + adjective" than B. The formula is pretty simple. The words for "more" and "less" are these:

Listen to Track 266

Más	More
Menos	Less

All you have to do is stick *más* or *menos* before the adjective (that's the word which describes a noun), then add *que*, meaning "than." Let's look at some examples:

Listen to Track 267

María es más elegante que Juan.	María is more elegant than Juan.
Ana es menos golosa que Ignacio.	Ana is less greedy than Ignacio.
Tu salud mental es más importante que este examen.	Your mental health is more important than this exam.
El Reino Unido es menos húmedo que Tailandia.	The UK is less humid than Thailand.
El libro es más gracioso que la película.	The book is funnier than the film.
Jorge es menos gruñón que su gemelo.	Jorge is less grumpy than his twin brother.

This formula also works for adverbs (words which describe verbs), as you can see here:

Listen to Track 268

Marta fights more bravely than her brother.	*Marta lucha más valientemente que su hermano.*
Today, they spoke less confidently than yesterday.	*Hoy hablaron menos confiadamente que ayer.*

Superlatives

Superlatives allow us to say that something is "the most + adjective" or "the least + adjective." All you have to do is add *el/la/los/las* before *más* or *menos*. You choose whichever one matches the noun and remember to make sure the adjective also agrees with the noun. Some examples will make it clearer.

Listen to Track 269

Jason is the funniest.	*Jason es el más gracioso.*
Caitlyn is the least tall.	*Caitlyn es la menos alta.*
My shoes are the shiniest.	*Mis zapatos son los más brillantes.*
My female cousins are the least annoying.	*Mis primas son las menos molestas.*

Top tip: To make something plural, you'll need to add *–s* or *–es*.

Irregular Stuff

As usual, you won't get away with learning Spanish without learning exceptions to the rules! There aren't too many to learn, but they are really common, so it's worth taking time to practice them.

Don't forget, we have these irregularities in English, too! You wouldn't describe something as "gooder" or "badder" than something else, you'd say "better" or "worse." The same kinds of words are irregular in Spanish.

Listen to Track 270

Good (well*)	*Bueno/(bien*)*
Better	*Mejor*
Best	*El/la mejor*

Bad (badly*)	Malo/(mal*)
Worse	Peor
Worst	El/la peor

*As well as adjectives, you may want to use comparatives and superlatives with adverbs. It's the difference between "you did a good job" and "you did the job well."

Listen to Track 271

Big (in the sense of "old," e.g. when talking about siblings)	Grande
Bigger (older)	Mayor
Biggest (oldest)	El/la mayor

Little (in the sense of "young," e.g. when talking about siblings)	Pequeño/a
Littler (younger)	Menor
Littlest (youngest)	El/la menor

Más de/Menos de

Listen to Track 272

So far, we've looked at *más* and *menos* with *que*. There are some occasions when you'll need to use *más de* or *menos de*. This is for when you're using numbers or quantities.

There will be more than 30 people.	Habrá más de 30 personas.
There will be fewer than 30 chairs.	Habrá menos de 30 sillas.

Phrases that use comparatives

There are several phrases that are super useful to know, and they all involve some form of comparison. Let's take a look:

Listen to Track 273

As ... as ...	Tan ... como ...
Victoria is as kind as Nacho.	Victoria es tan amable como Nacho.
Equally ...	Igual de ...
Victoria and Nacho are equally kind.	Victoria y Nacho son igual de amables.

The more ... , the more ...	Cuanto más ... , más ...
The more I work, the more money I earn.	Cuanto más trabajo, más dinero gano.

More and more	*Cada vez más*
I'm getting more and more excited.	*Me pongo cada vez más emocionada.*

As ... as possible	*Lo más ... posible*
Dress as smartly as possible.	*Vístase lo más arreglado posible.*

More than anything (i.e. mainly)	*Más que nada*
More than anything, I like rock music.	*Más que nada, me gusta la música rock.*

More or less	*Más o menos*
- How old are you? Like 40?	- *¿Cuántos años tienes? ¿40 o así?*
- Haha, more or less!	- *¡Jaja*, más o menos!*

*This is how Spanish speakers write "haha," which makes sense, because the Spanish "*j*" sound is quite like the English "h" sound! Jajaja.

Listen to Track 274

What a ... ...!	*¡Qué ... tan ...!*
What a beautiful dog!	*¡Qué perro tan bonito!*

To go from bad to worse	*Ir de mal en peor*
The situation has gone from bad to worse.	*La situación ha ido de mal en peor.*

To go from bad to worse / from the frying pan into the fire	*Ir de mal en peor.*
You're going from bad to worse with your grades!	*¡Con esas notas vas de mal en peor!*

Quiz time!

What better way to finish than to have a little practice?! Use the lesson above to help you translate the following sentences from Spanish into English. If you're feeling daring, try to translate the English phrases into Spanish, too!

In case you need it, this glossary has some of the words used in the context of the quiz!

Listen to Track 275

There is/there are	*Hay*
Adults	*Los adultos*
Children	*Los niños*
I have	*Tengo*
Money	*Dinero*
Than you	*Que tú*
He/she dances	*Baila*
Skillfully	*Habilidosamente*
I go out	*Salgo*
Frequently/frequency	*Frecuentemente/frecuencia*
Brave	*Valiente*
Selfish	*Egoísta*
But	*Pero*
Husband	*Marido/esposo*
Was	*Fue*
A day	*Un día*
I sing	*Yo canto*
Than her	*Que ella*
My brother	*Mi hermano*
Than me	*Que yo*
I want	*Quiero*
To see you	*Verte*
I saw	*Vi*
Cars	*Coches/carros*
Stubborn	*Terco (a)*
Your dad	*Tu papá*
House	*La casa*
Ready	*Listo (a)*
Exam	*Examen*

Quiz: Translate the following sentences into Spanish:

1. Tengo menos dinero que tú.

2. Carolina baila mejor que Juana.

3. Salgo menos frecuentemente que mi hermano.

4. Clara es la más valiente.

5. Miguel es el menos egoísta.

6. Soy una persona buena, pero mi marido es mejor.

7. Ayer fue un día malo. Hoy fue peor.

8. Yo canto mejor que ella.

9. Mi hermano es mayor que yo.

10. Más que otra cosa, quiero verte.

11. Vi más de 150 coches.

12. Juanca es menor que yo.

13. Eres tan terco como tu papá.

14. Se pone cada vez más y más difícil.

15. *La casa está más o menos lista.*

16. *¡Qué examen tan difícil!*

BONUS QUESTIONS:

17. Pedro dances more often than Laura.

18. I want to spend as much as possible.

19. Cristina is more important than him.

20. I understand Spanish better.

Well done for getting through the quiz – there were some tough ones in there! Here are the answers to the quiz:

1. I have less money than you.
2. Carolina dances more skillfully than Juana.
3. I go out less frequently than my brother.
4. Clara is the bravest.
5. Miguel is the least selfish.
6. I am a good person, but my husband is better.
7. Yesterday was a bad day. Today was worse.
8. I sing better than her.
9. My brother is older than me.
10. More than anything else, I want to see you.
11. I saw more than 150 cars.
12. Juanca is younger than me.
13. You're as stubborn as your dad.

14. It gets more and more difficult.

15. The house is more or less ready.

16. What a difficult exam!

17. *Pedro baila más seguido que Laura.*

18. *Quiero gastar lo más posible.*

19. *Cristina es más importante que él.*

20. *Entiendo mejor el español.*

Hopefully this has given you a solid basis for making comparisons in Spanish. Remember to make a daily learning habit – practice a little every day, and you should see your Spanish going *de bien en mejor*!

Workbook Lesson 22: Making comparisons – Hacer comparaciones

Exercise 1: Complete the sentences with comparative adjectives.

1- Mis hermanas son _____ (+ alto) que yo. (My sisters are taller than me.)
2- Yo bailo (+ bueno) _____ que ella. (I dance better than her.)
3- ¿Que país está (- poblado) _____ que la India? (Which country is less populated than India?)
4- ¿Qué es (+ malo) _____, estar enfermo o sin dinero? (What is worse, to be sick or without money?)
5- ¿Qué deporte es (- peligroso) _____, el esquí o el alpinismo? (Which sport is less dangerous, skiing or mountaineering?)

Exercise 2: Complete the sentences as in the example using: *viejo, caro, rápido, largo, capacidad.*

Example: Camilo mide 1.67, Pedro mide 1.70 (alto): Pedro es más alto que Camilo

1- Luisa tiene 19 años, María tiene 24 años: María es ____ ____ que Luisa. (Louisa is 19 years old, Mary is 24 years old: Mary is older than Louisa.)
2- Fresas 20 pesos el kilo, peras 15 pesos el kilo: las fresas son ____ ____ que las peras. (Strawberries 20 pesos per kilo, pears 15 pesos per kilo: strawberries are more expensive than pears.)
3- León 80 km/h, canguro 50 km/h: el león es ____ ____ que el canguro. (Lion 80 kph, kangaroo 50 kph: the lion is faster than kangaroo.)
4- Río Amazonas 6788 km, Río Danubio 2800 km: el río Amazonas es ____ ____ que el Danubio. (Amazon river 6,788 km, Danube river 2,800 km: the Amazon River is longer than the Danube.)
5- Toshiba 200 GB, Apple 300 GB: Apple tiene ____ ____ que Toshiba. (Toshiba 200 GB, Apple 300 GB: Apple has more capacity than Toshiba.)

Exercise 3: Tick the right answer.

1- Soy más fuerte _____ tú.
   a. que   b. quien
2- Este departamento es muy _____.
   a. antiguo   b. antigua
3- Esta casa es muy _____.
   a. baratas   b. barata

4- Esta falda es muy ____.
   a. corto b. corta

5- Este libro es aburrido, prefiero uno ____ ____.
   a. menos entretenido b. más entretenido

Exercise 4: Arrange the following words to create a correct sentence.

1- la más alta / Carla / es / de sus hermanas. (Carla is the tallest of her sisters.)
   _____

2- los más cómodos / los / son / mis zapatos. (My shoes are the most comfortable.)
   _____

3- de su familia / Soraya / es / la más cariñosa. (Soraya is the most loving of her family.)
   _____

4- las mejores / de la ciudad / son / estas naranjas. (These oranges are the best in town.)
   _____

5- el peor / libro / que he / leído / este es. (This is the worst book I've ever read.)
   _____

Exercise 5: Make superlative sentences as in the example.

Example: Pedro (chico + simpático): Pedro es el chico más simpático.

1- Julia (chica + alegre) _____. (Julia is the happiest girl.)

2- Regina (reloj + caro) _____. (Regina is the most expensive watch.)

3- Para mí, el café de Colombia (+ bueno) _____ del mundo. (For me, Colombian coffee is the best in the world.)

4- ¿Cuál es el país (+ interesante) _____ que has visitado? (Which is the most interesting country you've ever visited?)

5- El día de mi boda fue el (+ feliz) _____ de mi vida. (My wedding day was the happiest day of my life.)

Answers:

Exercise 1

1/ más altas. 2/ mejor 3/ menos poblado. 4/ peor 5/ menos peligroso.

Exercise 2

1/ más grande/grande 2/ más caras 3/ más rápido 4/ más largo 5/ más capacidad

Exercise 3

1/ que 2/ antiguo 3/ barata 4/ corta 5/ más entretenido

Exercise 4

1/ Carla es la más alta de sus hermanas. 2/ Mis zapatos son los más cómodos. 3/ Soraya es la más cariñosa de su familia. 4/ Estas naranjas son las mejores de la ciudad. 5/ Este es el peor libro que he leído.

Exercise 5

1/ Julia es la chica más alegre. 2/ Regina es el reloj más caro. 3/ Para mí, el café de Colombia es el mejor del mundo. 4/ ¿Cuál es el país más interesante que has visitado? 5/ El día de mi boda fue el más feliz de mi vida.

Conclusion

Learning grammar is not a walk in the park. So, if you were able to finish all of that by consistently learning every day, hats off to you! What an amazing job you did, you should be very proud.

If you were not able to follow the daily plan as suggested, don't despair. The important thing is you made use of this book to build a solid foundation in Spanish grammar.

We at My Daily Spanish hope that you will continue to keep learning every day. Even just a few minutes of daily study go a long way. It could be just listening to a 30-minute Spanish podcast, watching a Spanish movie or TV series, writing to a friend in Spanish, talking to a native Spanish speaker, or reading the news in Spanish... the list goes on.

We have other books available at the My Daily Spanish store (store.mydailyspanish.com) and on Amazon. Feel free to browse the different titles. They will help you solidify your knowledge of Spanish grammar.

If you have comments, questions or suggestions about this book, you may reach us at support@mydailyspanish.com or you can support it by leaving a review on Amazon. We'd be happy to hear from you.

You can also follow My Daily Spanish on social media, where we aim to give you fun and useful content to help you keep learning Spanish daily.

- Facebook (facebook.com/mydailyspanish)
- Instagram (@holamydailyspanish)
- Twitter (@mydailyspanish)
- Pinterest (pinterest.com/mydailyspanish)

And so with this, we say goodbye. It has been an awesome 22 days (or more!) with you. Keep learning Spanish!

Thank you,
My Daily Spanish Team

How to Download the Free Audio Files?

The audio files are in MP3 format and need to be accessed online. No worries though; it's easy!

On your computer, smartphone, iPhone/iPad, or tablet, simply go to this link:

https://mydailyspanish.com/grammar-beginner-audio

Be careful! If you are going to type the URL on your browser, please make sure to enter it completely and exactly. It will lead you to a wrong webpage if not entered precisely.

You should be directed to a webpage where you can see the cover of your book.

Below the cover, you will find two "Click here to download the audio" buttons in blue and orange color.

Option 1 (via Google Drive): The blue one will take you to a Google Drive folder. It will allow you to listen to the audio files online or download it from there. Just "Right click" on the track and click "Download." You can also download all the tracks in just one click—just look for the "Download all" option.

Option 2 (direct download): The orange button/backup link will allow you to directly download all the files (in .zip format) to your computer.

Note: This is a large file. Do not open it until your browser tells you that it has completed the download successfully (usually a few minutes on a broadband connection, but if your connection is slow it could take longer).

The .zip file will be found in your "Downloads" folder unless you have changed your settings. Extract the .zip file and you will now see all the audio tracks. Save them to your preferred folder or copy them to your other devices. Please play the audio files using a music/Mp3 application.

Did you have any problems downloading the audio? If you did, feel free to send an email to support@mydailyspanish.com. We'll do our best to assist you, but we would greatly appreciate it if you could thoroughly review the instructions first.

Thank you,

My Daily Spanish Team

About My Daily Spanish

MyDailySpanish.com is a website created to help busy learners learn Spanish. It is designed to provide a fun and fresh take on learning Spanish through:

- Helping you create a daily learning habit that you will stick to until you reach fluency, and
- Making learning Spanish as enjoyable as possible for people of all ages.

With the help of awesome content and tried-and-tested language learning methods, My Daily Spanish aims to be the best place on the web to learn Spanish.

The website is continuously updated with free resources and useful materials to help you learn Spanish. This includes grammar and vocabulary lessons plus culture topics to help you thrive in a Spanish-speaking location – perfect not only for those who wish to learn Spanish, but also for travelers planning to visit Spanish-speaking destinations.

For any questions, please email support@mydailyspanish.com.

Thank you,
My Daily Spanish Team

A Complete Audio Method for Spanish Language Learning

LEARN SPANISH
FOR BEGINNERS

A Complete Audio Method For Spanish Language Learning

By My Daily Spanish

Narrated by

- Jessica Del Cid
- Paul Solo
- Jose Noble

- Four weeks of easy-to-follow daily audio lessons
- Practical dialogues based on real-life scenarios
- 1,000+ most frequently-used Spanish vocabulary
- Speaking practice, quizzes, and review lessons

LEARN MORE

(https://geni.us/spanishlearning)

Printed in Great Britain
by Amazon